THE CRUSH-IT FORMULA

The CRUSH-IT Formula

Break Barriers, Maximize Potential and Achieve Elite Performance

Jaime Elizondo

©2025 All Rights Reserved. No portion of this book may be reproduced, stored in a retrieval system, or transmitted in any form or by any means—electronic, mechanical, photocopy, recording, scanning, or other—except for brief quotations in critical reviews or articles without the prior permission of the author.

Published by Game Changer Publishing

Paperback ISBN: 978-1-966659-58-7

Hardcover ISBN: 978-1-966659-59-4

Digital ISBN: 978-1-966659-60-0

www.GameChangerPublishing.com

DEDICATION

To my wife Aurelia for standing by my side through highs and lows, wins and losses, championships and losing seasons, for going on new journeys, and always embracing every move with joy and happiness. Thank you for your spirit, your patience, your kindness, your lightness, and your love. I am grateful for you.

To my incredible daughter Emilia, you inspire me every day to be even better. I dreamt of you forever, and you're finally here. I love you and am so proud of your strength, mindset, resilience, and willingness to let me coach, teach, and lead you. But most of all, for your love and kindness.

To my sisters—all of them—for their unconditional love and support. Yvonne, Rebecca, Liz, and Pat, thank you for teaching me in so many different ways. Yvonne, thanks for being my rock, my anchor, and for your unwavering support and belief. Rebecca, thanks for always being you and believing in me. Liz, you saved me in more ways than you know. And Pat, thanks for all the little notes and reminders of who I am and what I can accomplish. Luckiest brother in the world!

To my mom, you are and always have been my source of love and inspiration. You taught me how to love, be kind, and be compassionate, to live with grace and dignity, and to think of others before yourself. To my stepdad, thanks for being at every game and being my cheerleader. Thanks for taking a chance on us.

To all the players and coaches I was blessed to work with. Each and every one of you has made me the man I am today. You taught me more about myself, helped me develop my strengths, and inspired me to earn your trust daily, but most of all, I am grateful for the uniqueness of each one of you. Thank you for the moments of joy and happiness that can only be experienced by those inside the locker room and for sticking together through losses, tough seasons, and for your belief in me. I am blessed to have crossed paths with you, and I miss you "fellas" more than you know!

A special thank you to all of my friends, from El Paso to law school and everyone in between. I hope one day to earn the love and dedication you have shown me. And a very special thank you to Dennis Mikula. I love you, brother! Thank you for standing by my side—the world needs more of you!

Lastly, to my dad, "Papito" in heaven. I only knew you for a short period of time, but you live so strongly inside of me every day. I cannot wait to feel your hand on my face and hear your voice. If I have become half the man you are, then I did amazingly well. I miss you every day.

READ THIS FIRST

Just to say thanks for buying and reading my book, I would like to give you a free welcome call with me, no strings attached!

Scan the QR Code Here:

ACKNOWLEDGMENTS

"Jaime Elizondo was a pivotal figure in my career, not just as an Offensive Coordinator when we won the 2016 Grey Cup, but as a mentor who helped shape my mindset for success. His professionalism, attention to detail, and ability to instill a winning mentality were invaluable even when I was 41 years old, still competing at a high level and pushing myself to get the job done. His new book, The CRUSH-IT Formula, reflects the same principles he taught on the field: success isn't just about talent or circumstances, but the daily commitment to building the right mindset, habits, and leadership skills. If you are serious about unlocking your highest potential, this book is a must-read."

– Henry Burris
Assistant Head Coach, Offensive Coordinator, QB Coach
3x CFL Grey Cup Champion, 2x CFL MOP
Canadian Football Hall of Fame 2020

"Having coached and competed at the highest levels Coach Elizondo understands WINNING. Losing his DAD at an early age provided a BURN to tap into the POWER of ONE MORE DAY to drive him to CONTINUED ACTION and live to a STANDARD of Excellence. In his POWERFUL book, The CRUSH-IT Formula, he shares stories and the framework that encompasses all the aspects of what it TAKES to be a CHAMPION! READ IT."

– Ben Newman
USA Today TOP 5 Performance Coach
2x Wall Street Journal Bestseller

"I have known Jaime Elizondo for over 20 years. In this book, he draws from a lifetime of experiences to help those of us who never temper our passion to grow personally and professionally into the best version of ourselves each and every day. Through Jaime's personal life and professional journey through adversity and success, he has devised CRUSH-IT— a uniquely holistic formula for high-performance habits and personal growth. If you are a person who continuously and passionately desires to grow and improve, this read was built for you."

– **Marc Trestman**
Senior Offensive Assistant LA Chargers
Former NFL Head Coach Chicago Bears
Head Coach 3x Grey Cup Champion
2x CFL coach of the year
Adjunct Law Professor, University of Miami School of Law

"THE CRUSH-IT FORMULA is an inspiring and actionable guide to unlocking your highest potential. This book delivers a powerful framework rooted in resilience, discipline, and leadership qualities essential for success in any field. Whether you're a healthcare leader, business executive, or aspiring professional, the principles outlined here will help you push past limitations and achieve lasting excellence. This book masterfully blends mindset, discipline, and leadership into a powerful framework for success. Its insights resonate deeply, offering practical strategies to overcome obstacles, build resilience, and lead with purpose. This book will challenge and inspire you to elevate your performance and make a lasting impact. A must-read for anyone ready to take their performance to the next level!"

– **Deborah Visconi**
President and Chief Executive Officer,
Bergen New Bridge Medical Center
Top 25 People of Color Influencers
Top 25 Healthcare Influencers
Top 25 Women in Business

THE CRUSH-IT FORMULA

BREAK BARRIERS, MAXIMIZE POTENTIAL AND ACHIEVE ELITE PERFORMANCE

JAIME ELIZONDO

FOREWORD

I first met Jaime Elizondo in 2004 while coaching football at Hofstra University. At the time, I had already spent years immersed in the world of athletics, working with athletes who had the talent and drive to compete at the highest levels. But from the moment I met him, I knew I was in the presence of someone different. Someone who didn't just understand performance—he understood people. He has a rare ability to connect, challenge, and inspire in a way that makes those around him want to be better—not just in their sport, not just in their work, but in every aspect of their lives.

Over the years, I've seen countless coaches, trainers, and leaders come and go. Some are knowledgeable. Some are passionate. But very few possess the unique combination of insight, energy, and relentless commitment to excellence that defines Jaime. His approach to high performance isn't about temporary motivation or quick fixes. It's about transformation—the kind that leaves a lasting imprint, long after the final whistle blows or the workday ends.

One of the things that has always stood out to me about Jaime is his ability to see potential where others see limitations. He recognizes that greatness isn't just about talent—it's about mindset, preparation, and the willingness to embrace discomfort in the pursuit of something

bigger. He challenges those he works with to redefine their standards, to push beyond
self-imposed limits, and to commit to a process that demands both discipline and resilience.

As someone who has spent decades coaching and leading teams, I thought I had a firm grasp on what it takes to achieve success. But after working with Jaime, I realized there was another level—a level that I hadn't fully tapped into. His influence has changed the way I look at maximizing my own potential. He has helped me understand that elite performance isn't just about working hard; it's about working with intention, about refining the details, and about constantly evaluating and improving the processes that lead to success. His insights forced me to ask tough questions about my own habits, my own mindset, and my own ability to stretch beyond what I once thought was possible.

At the heart of his philosophy is *The CRUSH-IT Formula*—a proven system designed to help anyone reach the highest levels of performance in any field. This isn't just another motivational concept; it's a structured, actionable approach that breaks down the core principles of focus, preparation, execution, and resilience. Whether you're an athlete, a coach, a business leader, or a community leader, *The CRUSH-IT Formula* provides the blueprint for sustained excellence.

This book is for those who refuse to settle. Athletes will discover how to train their minds and bodies for peak performance. Coaches will learn how to instill a championship mindset in their teams. Business leaders will gain insight into building resilient, high-performing teams that thrive under pressure. And Community Leaders will see how these principles apply to creating lasting impact and inspiring those around them. No matter your role, if you're committed to growth, improvement, and making a difference, this book will give you the tools to reach the next level.

I've seen firsthand how these principles work. They've shaped championship teams, driven elite athletes to new heights, and helped leaders create cultures of success. More importantly, they're principles that anyone can apply—if they're willing to put in the work. This book isn't just about inspiration—it's about results. It's about taking the guesswork out of high performance and providing you with a step-by-step

FOREWORD

approach to breaking through barriers, unlocking your potential, and achieving things you never thought possible.

It's an honor to introduce you to the wisdom, experience, and proven strategies of Jaime Elizondo. As you turn these pages, be prepared to challenge your limits, embrace discomfort, and commit to the process of growth. Because with the right mindset, the right approach, and the right system, there are no limits to what you can achieve.

– Dennis Mikula, Jr.
President, Mikula Contracting, Inc. | Executive Board & Advisory Member, Multiple Leading Professional Organizations | 20+ Years Experience as Former College & High School Football Coach

CONTENTS

Introduction	xvii
1. Courage	1
2. Resilience	33
3. Unstoppable	67
4. Show Up	91
5. High Performing Habits	121
6. Internal Discipline	147
7. Tenacity	169
8. Crush-It As A Leader	181
Conclusion	201
Thank You For Reading My Book!	203

INTRODUCTION

Snow blanketed the ground, and the air stung with the biting chill of a cold, dreary day in Northern Canada. Thick clouds smothered the sun, casting a dull gray overcast that seemed to drain every ounce of vitality from the world. The cold felt sharper and harsher than usual, cutting through even the thickest layers.

The bleakness of the day mirrored the emptiness I felt inside. I had just watched my wife and three-year-old daughter leave for work and school. I was able to muster a smile for my little girl. She was overjoyed to have her daddy home after more than eight months of another coaching season; as their car disappeared, the silence settled around me like the snow outside. I stared out the window, feeling hollow, defeated, and hopeless.

This season was not like any other. Sure, I failed. There had been tough losses, hard-fought battles that did not go our way, and seasons where challenges seemed insurmountable. This one was different, however. It was not just tough; it felt soul-crushing. The weight of it pressed down on me relentlessly, like the heavy gray sky outside. I was crushed emotionally, mentally, and spiritually. The fire that had driven me for so long felt extinguished, leaving only ashes of doubt and despair.

The kind of defeat I felt was not just about the scoreboards or standings. It was more profound than that. It was the sense of letting down

INTRODUCTION

those who believed in me, my players, staff, my family, and myself. The unshakable confidence I once carried had eroded, replaced by a gnawing sense of inadequacy. As I stood there, staring blankly at the frozen world outside, the cold was not just seeping through the windows. It was inside me, festering, a chill I could not shake. I felt I had let down the coaches on our staff—Noel, Winston, Mac, Maxie, Vollono, Cam, Derek, Vincent, Rippon, and others. I felt I had let down my close friend, Brock Sunderland, the General Manager who hired me, believed in me, and remains a close friend to this day. Not to mention all the other coaches who had helped me prepare for this moment and been so instrumental in my development—Pete Mangurian, Marc Trestman, Rick Campbell, Bobby Dyce, Scott Milanovich, Doug Marrone, Jerry Glanville, Ron Rivera, Sean Payton, and so many others.

But most of all, I felt I had let down my friends and family—especially my wife, Aurelia, who had sacrificed so much, moved countless times and never stopped believing in me.

My entire career, I had worked for this opportunity—the chance to be a head coach in professional football—and it was gone. Over and done within a year. An opportunity that felt squandered, although I knew that wasn't the case. So many factors outside of my control had shaped my path, but as a coach and a leader, I took responsibility for all of them. I hated to admit it to myself, but I failed. The disappointment was just setting in.

We have all experienced that overwhelming disappointment that wraps itself around us and pulls us under. This kind of disappointment breaks us, challenging our ability to keep going, even at a basic level. All I ever wanted was to discover my true potential, push the boundaries, and see how far I could go. If I was going to lead a life I could be proud of, it had to be one where I reached my journey's highest heights possible.

As I sat there, staring out at the bleak expanse of never-ending drifts of snow, that same snow that the day before used to foster a warm sense of place, a curious single ray of sunlight broke through those oppressive clouds and that dreary white palette that silently taunted me. It was not much, mind you, just a fleeting glimmer cutting through the gray melancholy. However, it was enough to catch my attention and to remind me that this script could be flipped. At that moment, I knew, somewhere deep inside, that I would rise again. *Would*, *could*, and *should* came together. I knew there was so much more work ahead, but I also knew the spark existed, even if I could not fully grasp it that day.

I did not immediately latch onto that ray of sunlight and transform my mindset. This was not an instant epiphany or miraculous turning point. No, that beam of light was gone almost as quickly as it appeared, much like the hope it stirred within me. It was fragile and fleeting. The darkness still loomed, and I knew I was staring down days that would feel even heavier than this one.

What followed was not a quick or easy journey. It was a slow, often grueling process of self-examination, facing uncomfortable truths, and confronting the pain that had built up inside me. The path ahead required hard, unrelenting work. The kind of work that pushed me to my limits emotionally and mentally. That tiny spark, brief as it was, stayed with me. It was enough to remind me that even in the darkest moments, the possibility of light still could be shone on those who most need it. Little by little, that spark grew, fueling a determination to rebuild, understand, adapt, and find purpose again.

It was from those moments, those struggles, that this book was born. Every insight, tool, and piece of the framework you will encounter in these pages came from that long, painful climb out of the depths of a place we have all encountered, along with years of coaching and teaching others to be resilient, adapt, and how to win. This book results from that spark, fanned into a flame through persistence, reflection, and a refusal to give up.

If you are holding this book, perhaps you are also searching for your ray of light. Remember that even the faintest glimmer can lead to a new beginning if your eyes are open.

WHY YOU SHOULD READ THIS BOOK

My journey began with a single, unwavering goal: To rediscover how good I could be. That is it. Sounds simple. However, as we know, the simplest things usually become the most complex and difficult opponents. This effort was not about comparing myself to others or chasing external validation. Instead, it was about unlocking my potential, living

INTRODUCTION

fully into it, and finding joy. To be yourself is all that you can do. Yet, that question: *How good can I be?* continues to fuel and drive me today.

The pursuit of your utmost potential is never an easy road. It demands honesty, sometimes brutal honesty, about who you are and where you have fallen short. Along the way, you will encounter truths about yourself that are hard to face—moments when you were not your best, missteps that derailed you, failures that felt insurmountable, times when fear overshadowed courage, when weakness overtook resilience, and when you did not rise to the occasion. These moments are usually sobering and painful but are the crucible in forging growth.

This book is about our inevitable, challenging, and deeply human experiences. Yet, the focus is on confronting them, learning from them, and finding a way forward. It is about understanding that these moments do not define you. What defines you is your response. Through stories, insights, and a framework built from my journey, this book is an invitation to continue pushing forward and to keep reaching for the best version of yourself, even when the path is steep, and the setbacks feel overwhelming.

We have all had those moments that make us question whether we can accomplish more. The answer lies in the commitment to keep striving and learning and to never stop asking: "How good can I be?" That is where the magic happens. It is not in the perfection of the journey but in the perseverance to continue it. We have also faced situations that challenge our belief in our capabilities. The question is not whether you will have those moments but how you respond—what will you do next? This book invites you to embrace the discomfort, dig deep, and ask yourself, *How good can I be?* The answer lies not in what you have done so far but in the possibilities waiting for you when you refuse to give up.

In today's fast-paced, high-stakes society, the ability to perform at your best, whether as an individual, a team, or an organization, is not just an advantage but a necessity. Yet, for all the focus on performance, true mastery remains elusive. Why do some people and organizations thrive under pressure while others falter? What separates peak performers from the rest? Most importantly, how can you bridge that gap between high potential and elite performance?

Every day, we step onto the stage of life and perform, whether as an

INTRODUCTION

athlete striving for excellence, a CEO navigating the complexities of leadership, a manager guiding a team, or a parent nurturing the next generation. Performance is not limited to arenas, boardrooms, or offices; it is woven into the fabric of our daily lives. We perform when we show up for our families, take on challenges at work, and push ourselves to grow personally and professionally.

No matter the role, performance is about bringing the best of ourselves to each moment, no matter how big or small. For the athlete, it is about discipline and focus on the field. For the CEO, it is about decision-making, vision, and inspiring others. For parents, it is about balancing endless responsibilities while being present for the ones who matter most. Each of us has unique demands, but the need to perform unites us all, usually under pressure and often without recognition.

Performance isn't solely about the outcomes; it's about the process, the effort, and the intention we invest in the roles that define us. The reality is that there are times when we need to get things right. Some days, we fall short, and exhaustion and doubt take over. However, these moments offer the greatest chance for growth. How we react to setbacks, adapt, and keep moving forward ultimately shapes both our results and our character.

ABOUT ME

The pages ahead are designed to offer actionable insights for individuals and leaders who are ready to elevate their impact. Whether you are an athlete seeking a competitive edge, a professional aiming to excel in your career, or a leader striving to transform your team or organization, this book provides a roadmap to success. It is about cultivating the habits, mindsets, and systems that drive meaningful and sustainable progress.

A significant portion of this book's pages and soul comes from being in the arena, having faced the pressures of performing on some of the most prominent stages in the world. This book is driven by real-life experience, not theory. Having spent 22 years in professional football (playing, coaching, and leading some of the best athletes in the world) and now coaching the world's leading CEOs and working with organizations on driving elite performance, I have been able to push individuals from that dreaded word "potential" into elite action and performance. I share these experiences to show that the journey to elite performance is not exclusive to a few, but open to all willing to put in the work.

This book will focus on the CRUSH-IT formula (*Courage, Resilience, Unstoppable Show Up, High Performing Habits, Internal Discipline, and Tenacity*) a structured framework that helps individuals identify and overcome barriers, fostering meaningful and sustainable habit formation. *The CRUSH-IT Formula* is a set of principles and a powerful, transformative tool that can empower you to reach your full potential, both in your personal life and your career.

To make this concept even clearer, the book is divided into two key sections:

1. *The CRUSH-IT Formula* as it applies to leading in all aspects of your life, focusing on internal strengths and external impact, and how you can use this framework to enhance your personal growth and success.

2. *The CRUSH-IT Formula* as it applies to leadership, offering guidance on how to operate once you've reached a leadership position and how to navigate the challenges and responsibilities that come with it.

In developing this framework, I hope to plant a seed that you can nurture in limitless situations. When you finish this book, I encourage you to apply this acronym to other areas of life, discovering how powerful it can be in shaping your journey. This book is about practical application. It is a guide that equips you with the tools and mindset to uncover how good you can be in any situation. So, grab a cup of coffee, sit back, and discover how great you can be when you *CRUSH-IT!*

CHAPTER 1
COURAGE

It was a beautiful late November evening in Toronto, Canada. The temperature outside was hovering around 32 degrees Fahrenheit, and we were at BMO Field for the 2016 Grey Cup Championship. Yes, 32 degrees in Canada at this time of year is beautiful. I was walking on the field a couple of hours before the biggest game of my career. I served as the offensive coordinator for the Ottawa Red Blacks. In this game, we were massive underdogs against the Calgary Stampeders, who had the best record in a regular season in the 104-year history of the Canadian Football League (CFL).

Usually, two hours before the game, before we begin a structured warmup, coaches walk around and talk to one another while players go through their pre-game routine, listen to music, and prepare for what will be a terrific game. As I walked around, I felt confident and took it all in. After all, we had a great game plan, our team was prepared, and we had put in the work. Even though we were massive underdogs that day, a memory took me back to years before, to a conversation with a friend at a crucial juncture in my life almost 15 years prior. That's when the words "crush it" first surfaced.

Those 15 years ago, I had a decision to make. I had great opportunities to start working at big law firms in D.C. or take a job for $12,500 a year coaching football at the College of William & Mary. Preparing to make the three-hour drive from Washington D.C. to Williamsburg, Virginia, my friend was as excited for me as I was, and as he helped me go over last-minute interview scenarios, he said at the end, "You're ready. You're going to crush it." Although I had heard that expression before, I never really gave it much thought, and I could have never guessed that, years later, it would be the framework I would use while speaking on stages around the country, implementing it for teams and companies, and using it to help elevate individuals.

Back to the 2016 Grey Cup, I thought that we would crush it that night. Many talented football coaches dedicate decades to their craft without ever getting the opportunity to compete for, let alone win, a championship. As we got further into the pregame warmups, we were feeling terrific because we happened to have, at the time, the third all-time passing leader in professional football history, not just CFL history, but all of pro football—Henry Burris. Often affectionately called "Hank," he was a legend in the CFL. Hank had won two previous Grey Cup Championships. The Grey Cup in the CFL is the equivalent of the Super Bowl in the U.S. It is Canada's largest annual sports and television event, with the first Grey Cup played in 1909 (58 years before the first Super Bowl). He had been in these high-pressure environments, and like a wily vet, he knew precisely how to diminish the stress in these big moments. In addition to Hank, we had an incredibly talented receiving core, an athletic, intense, and gritty offensive line, a mix of power and finesse at running back, and a tough and nasty defense.

Structured pre-game warm-ups typically begin about one hour before a game and last roughly 30 minutes. In games like the Super Bowl or the Grey Cup, because of the pre-game shows, we have to be off the field earlier than usual, so we push the start of the pre-game back. After a quick team stretch, we break out into the individual portion of the warm-up, where we go into segments—routes on air (where only quarterbacks and receivers warm up,, skelly (similar to a game without the big guys, the offensive and defensive lines) versus the defense, a few team reps (where offense goes against defense), a few special teams plays (special teams involves the kicking game), and then off into the locker room where players and coaches make final mental preparations.

On this day, as we got into the skelly portion of the warm-up, I noticed that the backup quarterback, Trevor Harris, a heck of a player in his own right, was taking reps typically reserved for the starter. I saw Henry on a knee behind the action. I approached Hank and asked him, fittingly, "Are you ready to crush it?"

He looked at me and said, "Coach, I can't move."

I thought to myself, *This is classic Hank*. As I have witnessed countless times, he could ease the tension, relieve the pressure, and be his lighthearted self in the moment. Looking down at his eyes, I asked him, "What do you mean you can't move?" I saw something in his eyes that I had never seen before in him. I saw fear.

He looked me in the eye and said, "Coach, my knee is locked up; I can't move."

Trying to get clarity through the haze I was suddenly feeling, I asked him, "You mean you cannot run?"

He responded, "Coach, I cannot move."

At that moment, I felt the same fear I had seen in his eyes. You talk about going from getting ready to crush it to feeling crushed. Although I did not realize it at the time, that night set me down a path to figure out what it exactly means to *CRUSH-IT*, what it looks like on an everyday basis, what it embodies, and how to honestly look at success through a different lens, one that is not measured by results alone.

The principles around the CRUSH-IT model are designed as a tool and framework to help us unleash the mindset that allows us to rise to greatness. It serves as a step-by-step guide on how to do this and provides a formula for achieving it. We often need the proper criteria to evaluate success. The right metrics are crucial if we perform well, surpass expectations, and reach our potential. While we can see that other people are doing well, and while we may shine in specific areas, we still lack a true definition of what it means to excel. How can we guarantee that embracing certain principles or concepts will lead us to success?

Do you ever look at others and feel they are doing much better than you? Do you keep asking yourself questions such as:

- Why can't I get my act together?
- How do others do it?
- Why can't I find the discipline I need?
- How do they manage their time so effectively?
- What lets them be so bold?

- How do they bounce back so quickly?
- How do they have so much energy?
- What strategies do they use to stay organized?
- Do they have a routine that helps them stay focused?
- What motivates them to keep pushing forward?
- Are they prioritizing tasks differently than I am?
- How do they overcome distractions?
- What resources or tools do they use that I might not?
- Are they working harder, or are they just more innovative in their approach?
- What sacrifices are they making that I'm not?
- Do they have any support systems that help them succeed?

What if I told you that there is a way to ensure you are living your best life and that it is based on seven principles that are necessary ingredients for success? Furthermore, I can guarantee that you will be as successful as you want by living these principles daily. This framework, CRUSH-IT, provides that formula to help you understand if you are truly engaging in life and competing at your highest level. Let us dive into the first principle of that formula—courage.

When you go to the dictionary to define courage, you will find the following:

- Mental or moral strength to venture, persevere, and withstand danger, fear, or difficulty.
- The quality of mind or spirit that enables a person to face difficulty, danger, pain, etc., without fear; bravery.
- Strength in the face of pain or grief.
- The ability to control your fear in a dangerous or difficult situation.
- The ability to do something dangerous or to face pain or opposition without showing fear.
- A quality of spirit that enables you to face danger or pain without showing fear.

The most common denominator in the definitions above is fear. We all have experienced fear at some point, and for many of us, the weight on our backs or the anchor tied to our feet holds us back and prevents us from moving forward. We consider taking one step forward as we stand on the shore of opportunity. That anchor, fear, drags us back into the depths, keeping us from diving into the possibilities before us. Just as an anchor prevents a ship from moving freely, fear restrains us, limits us, and sometimes drowns us. Fear can make even the calmest waters seem treacherous. Yet many people argue that fear is a manufactured construct that served us years ago to protect us, but we have turned it into a self-serving tool.

The idea that fear is a construct, once valuable for survival but now manipulated for self-serving purposes, is a nuanced perspective supported by various experts. Originally, fear was crucial for survival, alerting humans to real threats and prompting life-saving responses. However, today, some argue that much of our fear is manufactured, driven by social and cultural influences rather than actual danger.

For instance, fear has historically helped us avoid life-threatening situations, but as society evolved, we have started creating false fears based on stereotypes, misinformation, and imagined threats. This kind of fear can divide people, prevent empathy, and lead to dangerous outcomes like violence or discrimination (psychologytoday.com). Modern-day fears, often stoked by media or political agendas, serve more to manipulate emotions and behaviors than to protect us (therapist.com). This shift suggests that fear, while still a vital human emotion, has become a tool for control in specific contexts, blurring the line between genuine survival instincts and artificial anxieties.

Whether it is a made-up construct or not, the feeling we experience of fear is real and limiting. If it were as easy to say that fear is a manufactured construct, and I need not worry about it anymore, then all of us would be further along than we are, and you need not read any further past this point. However, if fear and doubt about the unknown show up in your life and have consistently held you back from achieving the things you want, please keep reading. A lot of high performers I have worked with are not fearful, but doubt can be equally, if not more limiting, than fear.

Growing up as a boy in El Paso, Texas, I came to understand fear at a young age. Although I spent my childhood in West Texas, I was born in Aguascalientes, Mexico, a city situated in the heart of the country. Its name, Aguascalientes, translates to "hot waters."

I never knew my father—he passed away when I was just six months old. Even so, I feel his absence every day, and I would give anything to hear his voice or feel his touch, even just once. But more on that later. When my dad died, my mom was left to raise me and my sister, who was only about 18 months old at the time. With two children under two, my mother had no choice but to "figure it out." I imagine it took immense courage.

It was then that we moved back to Ciudad Juárez, where my grandparents lived, and settled into their home. At the time, this kind of multigenerational living arrangement was common, a way for families to support one another through life's uncertainties. My grandfather, a highly respected and well-known doctor in Mexico, became the cornerstone of our stability. His presence provided not just financial security but also wisdom, guidance, and a sense of continuity in an otherwise shifting world.

For a while, it felt as though we had found solid ground. But that stability was fleeting. Just a year later, my grandfather passed away, and with him, the foundation we had come to rely on began to crack. His loss was more than just the absence of a beloved family figure, it was the unraveling of the sense of security he had built for us. In many ways, his passing marked the beginning of another period of uncertainty, one that would shape our family's journey in ways we couldn't yet foresee.

My first experience with both fear and courage came through the eyes of my mom. After much insistence from others, she decided to open her heart again, cautiously stepping into the world of dating. Eventually, she considered remarriage, a decision that would redefine our lives. For my sister and me, the day she remarried marked a turning point, a shift from the familiarity and comfort of our grandparents' home to an entirely new reality.

Suddenly, we found ourselves leaving behind everything we had known, moving across the border to El Paso, Texas, into a small two-bedroom apartment with a man who, at the time, was a stranger to us. My stepdad did the best he could, he provided a home, stability, and his manner of showing love. I can still picture him on the sidelines at every football, baseball, basketball, or soccer game I played in, always cheering me on. He continues to be one of my biggest supporters to this day.

Not many people would take on the responsibility of raising two young kids who weren't their own, and for that, I respect him. But the transition wasn't easy for my sister and me. We had to adjust to a new home, new rules, and the presence of someone who, while well-intentioned, wasn't the father we had once known. It was a time of uncertainty, but also a time that taught me that courage isn't just about taking risks—it's about adapting, growing, and learning to embrace change, even when it feels uncomfortable.

My love and respect for my mom are beyond words. She managed to raise three kids with unwavering strength and grace, stretching just $200 every two weeks to cover groceries, clothes, shoes, school supplies, and everything else we needed. Somehow, she made the impossible work—turning scarcity into sufficiency, making sure we never felt the full weight of our struggles. While my dad didn't make the same sacrifices, she never let that stop her from giving us the best she could. She always found a way to save, even when there was nothing extra, setting aside just enough for one more Christmas gift, making sure we never felt less than any other kids. She sacrificed her own wants without hesitation, skipping new clothes or simple luxuries so we wouldn't go without.

I admire her resilience, her quiet determination, and the love she poured into every meal, every scraped-together school outfit, and every moment she reassured us that we would be okay. She taught me the true meaning of strength—not just in surviving hard times but in doing so with love, dignity, and an unbreakable spirit.

On my first day of kindergarten, I knew very little English. I clearly remember the feeling of fear taking hold, even if, at four years old, I couldn't fully understand what it was. I just knew it wasn't a good feeling. It wasn't the first time I experienced fear, nor would it be the last. At that age, I had no concept of courage or what it meant, but as I grew, I became more familiar with it. Courage would go on to play a recurring role throughout my life.

El Paso is a city in the westernmost part of Texas, so far west that many Texans considered El Paso a part of New Mexico. It is on the U.S.-Mexico border directly across from Ciudad Juarez. It is known for its unique blend of cultures, reflecting a rich combination of Mexican, Native American, and Texan heritage. At the time, there was a minor league baseball team, The El Paso Diablos, and the university sports teams at the University of Texas, El Paso (UTEP), the Miners.

Several times a year, the rodeo would come to town, and while I loved the energy, the competition, and the thrill of every event, nothing fascinated me more than the professional bull riders. That was when I first understood what courage looks like. To a little boy, the mere thought of climbing onto a bucking bull and holding on for eight seconds seemed like the ultimate test of bravery, so much so that years later, I bought a Professional Bull Riders Association jacket as a tribute to that admiration. It might have been the ugliest jacket ever, but I wore it with pride.

Somewhere along the way, during one of our many moves, that awful-looking jacket mysteriously disappeared. My wife, Aurelia, who I love dearly, once joked, "It must have been stolen." Whether it was or not, the memory remains. I would sit in the stands, watching those riders battle to stay on those angry-as-hell bulls, and I'd think to myself, *That guy is so courageous. I hope I can have that kind of courage someday.*

Courage holds different meanings for different people. For some, it's about confronting their fears and stepping into discomfort and uncertainty. Others define it as pushing beyond their comfort zone or tackling difficult conversations and tough decisions. For many, courage is acknowledging doubts, insecurities, and the unknown while choosing to move forward anyway. What does courage mean to you? Take a moment and write your definition of courage down on the side of the text or in your journal. How we define courage is important, and we will come back to your definition later.

Fear and courage are deeply intertwined as they often exist in a delicate balance. Fear can act as a catalyst for courage, pushing us to confront challenges that might otherwise overwhelm us. When we feel fear, it highlights what truly matters to us, motivating us to take action despite our apprehensions. Courage is not the absence of fear; instead, it is the ability to face it head-on. When we act despite our fears, we strengthen our resilience and grow. Each time we confront fear, we build a foundation of courage, creating a cycle where facing one leads to developing the other. Together, they form a powerful dynamic that drives personal growth and transformation.

Before we dive deeper, let me clarify the difference between courage and bravery. Courage involves facing fear, uncertainty, or danger, often when one has time to assess the risks and still choose to move forward. It is more about mental or emotional strength and usually involves a fierce internal battle. Conversely, bravery implies immediate action in danger or challenge, often without hesitation or fear. It is more instinctual and can be seen as boldness in the moment. Usually, bravery carries a physical or visible act of heroism. I equate it this way. Deciding to become a bull rider takes courage; it is a conscious decision made ahead of time, knowing the risks and possible consequences. Bravery is getting the hell out of the way after the bull has thrown you off and is charging full speed ahead at you! That is a pain I would more than gladly avoid.

So, let us dig a little deeper. Before we can genuinely take that first step, it is crucial to recognize a few key elements. First, we must ask ourselves: "What exactly am I afraid of, and what pain am I trying to avoid?" Fear is always linked to preventing pain. Most folks do not enjoy pain; it is uncomfortable and unwelcome, so we naturally gravitate toward comfort and ease.

True growth happens when we resist the temptation to take the easy path and accept that challenges and discomfort are part of the journey. Instead of avoiding these pain points, we should confront them directly. Identifying the specific challenges we're avoiding is crucial. Embracing discomfort is never easy, but it is an essential step for growth. It requires being open to change and recognizing that the road to success is often lined with moments of discomfort. Most of us know this, but we still sit back and hesitate when faced with uncertainty. We cling to familiarity, fearing failure, rejection, or the possibility of falling short. But true progress comes when we push past those fears, taking action despite the discomfort. It's in those difficult moments when we feel like retreating, that real transformation happens.

Growth demands resilience, self-awareness, and the willingness to embrace the unknown. It means choosing to show up every day, even when it's hard, even when doubt creeps in. The path forward is never without obstacles, but those who succeed are the ones who lean into the struggle, knowing that every challenge is an opportunity to learn, adapt, and become courageous.

So instead of sitting back, waiting for the perfect moment, we must take the first step, no matter how uncertain or uncomfortable it may feel. Because in the end, it's not just about reaching our goals—it's about who we become along the way.

CATEGORIZING YOUR FEARS

Recognizing and organizing our fears can be a valuable skill. It provides a sense of control and helps us manage our emotions more effectively. While we all experience a range of concerns, nearly all fears can be grouped into five main categories: fear of failure, fear of rejection, fear of the unknown, fear of loss, and fear of regret. These core fears often hold people back from taking action in life. These fears can create mental and emotional obstacles, limiting personal growth and opportunities. Breaking free from these fears requires cultivating courage, building self-awareness, and reframing fear as an opportunity for growth. By facing fears head-on, individuals can unlock their potential and take meaningful action in life.

Andy Frisella, the author of the bestselling book *75 Hard* and *Mental Toughness*, details how prevalent the fear of failure is in individuals. He found that of every 100 people, approximately 70 will give up before attempting a task outside of their routine due to their intense fear of failure. I phrase it as "the start becomes the stop." The starting line is what stops 70 percent of people. Frisella adds that out of the remaining 30 percent, 20 percent will give up at the first challenge—quit at the first obstacle. Eight of the last 10 percent will stop when faced with significant difficulties or major roadblocks. This leaves two people, and this is where the notion of two percent comes from. Two percent of the people make it to their goal. I bring this in because I firmly believe that those two percent were every bit as afraid of failing as others at some point.

However, they faced those failures and moved past them. They crushed those fears.

∼

It was a sunny Sunday morning and the air was filled with the smell of freshly cut grass. I had just finished mowing our backyard on a hot July morning. My daughter was in the yard, her normal whirlwind of energy, as she explored our new ninja warrior obstacle course. As I glanced over, I saw her with a worried look on her face as she was looking at the climbing ropes. I asked, "Are you thinking about climbing the ropes?" She looked at me with a look of anguish, a look that said, *I'm not sure.* After a minute, she said, "I can't." There are a few words that aren't allowed in our house, and at the top of that list are the words *I can't.* Reminding my daughter about those words, I also asked her what advice she would give me if I were in the same situation. Straightening up, pulling her shoulders back, putting her coaching look on, and tapping into her coaching voice, she said, "Daddy, face your fears. If you want to be great, you have to face your fears." She was right. Each small victory over fear builds momentum, paving the way for greater achievements and deeper fulfillment. Fear may always exist, but it's how you respond to it that defines who you become.

THE FIVE FEARS

1. Fear of Failure

The fear of failure, also known as **atychiphobia**, is an intense emotional response to the possibility of not succeeding in a task, goal, or endeavor. This fear often goes beyond simple anxiety about disappointing outcomes; it can significantly affect one's behavior, mindset, and life decisions. Atychiphobia comes from the Greek word meaning "unfortunate." People with atychiphobia may avoid any situation where they see a potential for failure, such as an exam or job interview. It can also mean being afraid of a failed relationship, a failed career, or being a disappointment to others. For most people, this fear of failure shows up in a variety of ways:

- anxiety, worry, or panic about trying something new
- procrastination
- avoiding opportunities that carry risks
- overthinking possible negative outcomes
- catastrophic thinking
- chronic worry

When I wrote this book, the 2024 Olympics were occurring. Hundreds of athletes competed, laid it on the line, and faced their fear of failing. What comes to mind when you think of the few who experience the joy of standing atop the podium and having a medal placed around them? I think of the courage it took to fight all those battles physically, mentally, and emotionally. It is not just the hours of physical training; it is the moments when it became too hard, where they wanted to tap out, and they wondered why they were doing this when the mental chatter told them they were not good enough.

I think about how they overcame their fear of failing, of laying it all out on the line for the world to see, knowing that they might not make it to the top—might not even place. I love these moments because it is in these moments that we either tap into our courage or listen to that little voice that is stronger than anything else, that screams at us at times, *You can't. You are not good enough. You will fail.* Yet, there are great examples of people who have overcome tremendous odds, come from many backgrounds and challenging situations, and overcome injuries, sicknesses, illnesses, mental doubt, and so much more to compete at these Olympics. The one common denominator in all of this is courage. Courage to fail.

∼

Actionable Tips to overcome fear of failure:

- **Reframe failure as feedback.** EVERYTHING is seen as feedback. I don't believe in the saying we either win or we learn. No. We *fail*, and that's how we get the needed feedback on what went wrong, how we adjust, and what we

need to do differently next time. And when we win, we also learn if we analyze what we did that led to victory.
- **Shift your perspective.** One of the best tools to use here is the Best Case/Worst Case/Most Probable Case Model: By going through the Best Case/Worst Case scenarios—and taking it to completion—shifts our perspective. Here's a brief example:

Client: I am afraid if I leave my job and pursue my dream that I might fail and lose the security I have. And what if I fail? What if the business never takes off?
Me: What would happen if the business never takes off?
Client: Then I can't provide for my family.
Me: Then what happens?
Client: My wife leaves me. I have to sell the house, and I lose all my savings.
Me: And when your wife leaves you, and you lose all your savings, what happens next?
Client: I lose custody of the kids, and they think I am a deadbeat dad because I have to move back in with my mom.
Me: So you move in with your mom. Then what happens?
Client: I can't find a job, I start drinking, my mom kicks me out, and I find myself living on the streets.
Me: And then?
Client: I become a drug addict, and I die a slow, painful death, lonely, and even my dog leaves me (you get the picture).
Me: Now, what is the probability of you starting a business, failing, and you dying a slow, painful, lonely death on the corner of 5th and Main?
Client: .0000000001 percent.

Then, we do the same with Best Case and Most Realistic. It helps put things in perspective.

- Approach things from a growth mindset (more to come on that)

- Build a team around you for support (asking for help is one of the hardest things to do for many but is a huge part of resilience. We will address this in the chapter on resilience.)
- Take action in the face of fear. Simple—take action! The more action you take, the more you overcome your fears. Let me say it again: take action.
- Celebrate the effort and not just results. Acknowledge and reward yourself for trying. Focus on effort and progress.

2. Fear of Rejection

Fear of rejection. We all have it. Some people have overcome this, others are still held back by it. This fear centers around the worry of not being accepted by others, whether in personal relationships, social situations, or professional settings. It has evolutionary roots; it is what lets us survive and evolve as a species. This is the fear of being excluded, judged, or turned away by others. It often stems from a deep desire for acceptance and belonging. This fear focuses on how others perceive and respond to you. Nonetheless, it is powerful and causes us to change how we show up or fail to show up. Oftentimes, it prevents us from reaching out and making meaningful connections or being bold and pursuing our dreams for fear that we need more to offer. All of us—every single one of us—has faced this fear at some point in our lives, but for some, this shows up more powerfully than others. When I first started writing this book, I realized this was the fear that was holding me back and limiting thoughts such as, *What if the book does not resonate? What if there are not enough relatable stories? Who wants to hear my story anyway?* So I delayed and delayed, and it was not until I reframed rejection that I moved forward.

Like so many people, I have felt this same fear multiple times. *What if they don't think I'm good enough? What if others think of me in a certain way? What if I am not accepted?* This fear of rejection and not being accepted is a concern that exists in all of us. More often than not, it inhibits us from moving forward. We sit back and play small because we are afraid to fully put ourselves out there and envision our lives on fire. So, take the courageous step of embracing the highest vision of yourself. Rather than seeing rejection as a measure of my worth, I began to view it as an opportunity to share my challenges and approach my journey with openness, honesty, and transparency.

I haven't always had it all figured out. In fact, there were many times I struggled—whether in my relationships, at work, with self-discipline, or in overcoming limiting beliefs. I didn't feel extraordinary or as though I had achieved anything remarkable enough to write a book. But that was precisely why I needed to do it. If you've ever felt stuck or as if you're not reaching your full potential, know you're not alone—I've been there too. Many of us share this journey of facing challenges and finding a way forward. My story is proof that breaking free and rising to new heights is possible. Within these pages, you'll find relatable experiences and practical insights designed to inspire and guide you on your own path to success. The CRUSH-IT framework serves as a step-by-step roadmap—not just for getting unstuck but for transitioning, creating, and tapping into the courage that already lies within you.

Actionable Tips to overcome fear of failure:

- Accept it and remind yourself that others have experienced it.
- Understand that it's part of your DNA. This is evolution, and it has protected you. Just don't let it cocoon you.
- Validate your feelings. Don't negate or run from them. Embrace them and understand that rejection is tough.
- Desensitize yourself to rejection. Intentionally put yourself in positions where you might hear a "no." Over time, you will become more comfortable.
- Seek validation from YOURSELF and your actions. Although acceptance is needed, redirect your focus from what others think of you or about you to what YOU THINK OF YOU.
- Understand where the fear is coming from.
- Limit negative self-talk.

3. Fear of the Unknown

The third thing many of us fear is the unknown. Fear of the unknown is the apprehension or anxiety we feel when faced with uncertainty or unfamiliar situations. It stems from our innate need for predictability and control. When we cannot foresee outcomes or fully understand what lies ahead, our minds often fill the gaps with worst-case scenarios or exaggerated risks, amplifying our discomfort. Uncertainty about the future can be daunting, but it is powerful enough to cement us into the place we are at. It makes it nearly impossible to embrace new opportunities or experiences. It keeps you in relationships you should not be in, personally and professionally, and it goes against everything society teaches us today: comfort, the path of least resistance, and ease.

The problem is not only society but our hard-wiring, as well. A study by Richard Bagozzi and Utpal Dholakia (presented in the article *Goal Setting and Goal Striving in Consumer Behavior*) explored how individuals tend to choose paths of least resistance in goal-directed behavior to conserve cognitive resources (sagejournals.com). At its core, fear of the unknown arises because humans are wired to seek safety and avoid potential danger. However, it can also be a barrier to growth, as many of life's most meaningful experiences require us to embrace uncertainty.

We crave and want it, yet this need for certainty plunks us down right where we are, stuck, glued to the toilet seat. It causes us to doubt, delay, procrastinate, and justify our inaction with excuses, so we latch back on to what we know, even if it holds us back or no longer serves us. The comfort of familiarity becomes a prison, preventing us from taking the risks that lead to growth and change.

Imagine you are eagerly waiting to hear back from a potential employer about an exciting job offer. Your interviewer was hard to read, leaving you with no clues about the outcome. As the days pass, you find yourself wishing to know the result, good or bad, just to escape the torturous waiting. Now, think back to when you were dating—for some, that's right now. Wouldn't it be better if someone told you right away that they were not interested in seeing you again rather than leaving you anxiously checking your phone for a message? Would you even consider risking your pride by asking for clarity on their feelings, even if the timing seemed off? What about that offer you made on a house? Waiting for hours to know if it was accepted. What about the proposal you submitted? Would it be the one chosen? What will happen when I move in with my boyfriend? What if I cannot play in this game? Will my position be secure?

The fear of the unknown can be psychologically draining. In all these situations, the uncertainty creates a sense of discomfort that can be difficult to bear. It holds us in check, keeps us in a safe spot, and allows us years later to look back and say, "Why didn't I...?"

Actionable steps to help with Fear of the Unknown:

- Visualize positive outcomes. We often focus on the negative aspects of the unknown. Force yourself to focus on the positive possibilities and visualize those outcomes.
- Focus on the journey, your effort, and not the result.
- Find joy in embracing the unknown. Let go of the need to control the outcome and instead focus on the adventure it brings.
- Close the knowledge gap. Unknown is usually tied to a lack of information. Ask questions, talk to others, and research, so that you can gain clarity and reduce uncertainty. The more you understand, the less intimidating the unknown becomes, empowering you to make informed decisions and take confident steps forward.

4. Fear of Loss

The fourth fear is the fear of loss. Whether it's the fear of losing loved ones, health, financial stability, reputation, or opportunities, this fear can be emotionally crippling. It often leads to a protective mindset, where individuals cling tightly to what they have, hindering their ability to fully engage with life or pursue their goals with genuine commitment. This fear shows up in ways that affect our decisions, holding us back from taking risks or stepping into the unknown.

As responsibilities grow, this fear often intensifies. The stakes become higher—career success, family well-being, financial security, and personal reputation all seem more precarious when tied to our actions. For leaders, this fear is particularly burdensome, as their choices impact not only themselves but also the people they lead. I've felt this acutely in my leadership career, whether as a head coach or in other roles. The fear of making decisions that might harm those under my guidance has been both a motivator and a weight. It was a constant mental tug-of-war between doing what was safe and what was necessary for growth.

The fear of loss often intertwines with the fear of regret. The anxiety of potentially losing something valuable—opportunities, respect, or relationships—fuels our worry about looking back with remorse. It compels us to stick with the familiar, even when it no longer serves us. In leadership, this can manifest as avoiding tough decisions or delaying necessary actions for fear of the fallout. Yet, ironically, the very act of clinging to the status quo often leads to the regret we hoped to avoid.

When we step into leadership, whether in our professional or personal lives, we must confront the fear of loss directly. It requires courage to embrace uncertainty and make bold decisions, even when the stakes are high. True leadership lies not in avoiding loss but in navigating it with integrity, purpose, and a focus on the bigger picture.

5. Fear of Regret

Fear of regret is a powerful and often subconscious force that shapes our decisions, relationships, and life choices. It is the emotional distress that comes from imagining a future in which we look back with disappointment at a choice we made—or failed to make. Unlike other common fears such as failure, rejection, or the unknown, the fear of regret is unique because it is future-oriented, meaning it is driven by anticipation rather than immediate consequences

Psychologists often describe this fear as an extension of loss aversion, a cognitive bias where the pain of losing something is felt more intensely than the joy of gaining something of equal value. This causes people to avoid risks or decisions that may later bring feelings of remorse, even if they have a strong rational basis for moving forward. This is why I mention that Fear of Loss and Fear of Regret are closely linked.

This fear is powerful, as we are often caught up in the following.

The Illusion of a Perfect Choice – Many people believe that there is a singular "right" choice in life and that every decision should lead to the best possible outcome. This perfectionist mindset amplifies the fear of making a wrong decision.

Emotional Overestimation – People often assume that regret will feel worse than it actually does. Research shows that, over time, individuals adapt to their choices, but fear tricks the mind into thinking regret will be unbearable.

Missed Opportunities Seem Larger in Retrospect – When we look back, we tend to romanticize what "could have been," often ignoring the struggles and difficulties that the alternative path might have carried.

Social and Cultural Conditioning – Society often reinforces the fear of regret through sayings like "You'll regret it if you don't try" or "You only live once." While these statements can be motivating, they can also create pressure to avoid making decisions that could later be questioned.

While it seems natural to avoid actions that may lead to regret, constantly fearing it can lead to:

- Decision Paralysis – Overthinking and second-guessing every decision, making it difficult to take action.
- Missed Opportunities – Choosing inaction over potential risk, leading to stagnation in personal and professional life.
- Diminished Confidence – A persistent fear of regret can erode self-trust, making people overly dependent on external validation.

This is where the fear of regret becomes a powerful motivator. At the end of our lives, we won't reflect on the possessions we kept or the comfort zones we maintained. Instead, we'll think about the risks we took, the people we loved, the adventures we embraced, and the difference we made. Regret stems not from failure or loss but from not trying —failing to take the chances that could have led to growth and fulfillment.

For me, this realization was pivotal. I've had my share of regrets, but I've come to understand that the power to shape our future lies in the choices we make today. By confronting the fear of loss and stepping boldly into uncertainty, we can create a life where regret takes a back seat to fulfillment. It's not about avoiding all mistakes, but about aligning our actions with our values and aspirations, knowing that even setbacks can serve as stepping stones to something greater.

Our fears—especially the fear of loss—show up in our behaviors and decisions. They can either paralyze us or propel us forward. The mindset we choose to adopt is everything. The first step is to face these fears, understand their impact, and decide to move forward anyway. It's in this act of courage that we begin to transcend the fear of loss and avoid the regret of not having lived fully.

Actionable Steps

- Embrace loss as part of risk and chasing your dreams. In football, there was nothing worse than losing in the championship game. I was fortunate to win one but lose two others. Some people say it's better not to make it than to lose in the championship, but they're wrong. I will always choose the chance to lose if it means competing and having a chance for extraordinary performance…and a chance to win.
- Know your limits. Figure out what you're willing to give up, then take a good look at yourself and ask: What is it about those things that is so important to you that they might impede your growth?
- Have backup plans: As a play caller, I always prepared two call sheets: one tailored for the starter and another specifically for the backup quarterback. This wasn't due to a lack of trust in either player, but rather a reflection of intentional planning and strategic foresight. Each quarterback brings unique strengths, skills, and experiences to the field, and having a separate plan ensured that we could maximize their potential while adapting to the dynamic needs of the game.

The starter's call sheet was often designed around a broader set of plays, incorporating their familiarity with the system and ability to execute a wider range of options. For the backup, the call sheet focused on plays that matched their skill set and comfort level, emphasizing efficiency and confidence-building to set them up for success in high-pressure moments.

This approach wasn't just about preparation—it was about leadership and adaptability. By having tailored plans, I could instill confidence in the backup quarterback, signaling that their contributions were equally valued and accounted for. It also reduced hesitation and second-guessing during critical moments in a game, enabling me to make clear, decisive calls when circumstances changed unexpectedly.

Planning for contingencies like this is a cornerstone of effective leadership—not just in football but in any high-stakes environment. It's about recognizing the value of preparation, trusting the people around you, and being ready to adapt when the game doesn't go according to the original plan.

- Reverse the question: What am I going to lose by *not* doing this? And at 90 years old, am I going to look back with regret? Answer honestly.

The Cycle of Pain and Fear: How They Feed and Reinforce Each Other

Fear is always tied to pain. It is not necessarily physical pain but pain of discomfort or psychological pain. Our brain is wired to avoid pain. The relationship between psychological pain and fear often forms a negative self-reinforcing loop that can paralyze decision-making and prevent us from taking action. Frequently, we must dig deeper into the past because this is not physical pain but emotional pain. It originates in many ways but can come from past experiences, regrets, or even a sense of inadequacy. Fear amplifies this pain, focusing the mind on potential risks and possible failures, making even small challenges seem daunting.

Reading this chapter might've brought up some stuff for you. Maybe you remembered something from the past, and your heart started racing, or you felt nervous and got butterflies in your stomach or sweaty hands as you read the paragraphs above. Many of you probably had some physical reactions. Some of it might have come from a fear of facing past pain or something you've been avoiding. If you've gone through rejection, failure, or loss before, the thought of experiencing something similar again feels like reliving the pain. This makes you more sensitive to potential pain and creates a fear of messing up, being judged, or facing the unknown, which holds you back and stops you from moving forward. Basically, fear becomes a way to protect yourself from emotional pain, even if it means missing out on personal growth or opportunities. It happens to a lot of us almost every day.

This connection between pain and fear often triggers overthinking, limiting beliefs, negative self-talk, and doubt. The brain's tendency to prioritize safety and minimize risk can make the pain-fear loop all-consuming, blocking any sense of progress and preventing us from operating from the PFC of our brain, the area responsible for creativity, problem-solving and, most importantly, rational thinking. However, recognizing and reframing these feelings can gradually break the cycle, allowing fear to be acknowledged rather than avoided and opening up room for action and resilience. At this point, I urge you to pause and reflect. What are you fearing, and what pain are you really avoiding? This reflection can deepen your understanding of your fears and enhance self-awareness, transforming your approach to fear and pain into a doorway to success rather than a barrier blocking your path. Before we go further, let's break down the types of pain that we tend to avoid.

THREE TYPES OF PAIN: CHALLENGE, SACRIFICE, AND OUTCOME

When we study behavior, one thing becomes clear: our brains are hardwired to avoid pain. Whether consciously or subconsciously, we tend to steer clear of hardship, doing everything in our power to delay it or avoid it entirely. This instinctual aversion often plays a significant role in the decisions we make—or don't make—and it shapes how we approach growth, change, and success. Let's explore the three types of pain that most often hold us back.

1. The Pain of Challenge

The first and perhaps most common type of pain we avoid is the pain of challenge—the discomfort of pushing ourselves beyond our current limits. This is the pain of stepping into uncharted territory, where growth begins. The problem is that this "perceived" pain often paralyzes us before we even start. Just the thought of how hard something might be—whether it's starting a new fitness routine, launching a business, or having a tough conversation—can feel so daunting that we never take the first step.

This avoidance is understandable. After all, the pain of challenge is immediate, tangible, and uncomfortable. Yet, what lies on the other side of avoiding it is even worse: the pain of regret. Regret is that lingering ache we feel when we look back and realize we didn't try, didn't push, or didn't give our best effort. The reason we often choose to avoid challenges is because the pain of regret doesn't show up right away—it's a bill we don't realize we've accrued until it's too late to pay.

I am passionate about helping others move past this type of pain because I know, as you do, that what lies on the other side of challenge is far greater than any momentary discomfort. It's progress, growth, and fulfillment. And avoiding that pain, while seemingly easier, comes with a cost most of us cannot afford.

2. The Pain of Sacrifice

Next is the pain of sacrifice—the fear of losing something valuable in pursuit of something else. It's the inner dialogue that whispers, *If I do this, I might lose that. If I don't, I might lose something else.* These trade-offs are unavoidable, and the decisions can be incredibly tough. For many, the perceived price of sacrifice feels too high, and they stop themselves before they truly begin.

Let's be honest: achieving extraordinary success or elite performance requires sacrifices. Whether it's time, comfort, social life, or even financial security, the path to greatness demands giving up certain things to gain others. But there's no shame in deciding that the cost isn't worth it. That choice simply clarifies what you truly value and what you're willing to accept—and that's okay.

However, it's also true that the gap between high potential and elite performance often lies in what you're willing to give up. For me, failing to realize my full potential is a punishment I'm unwilling to face—a pain I refuse to endure. Sacrifices, while difficult, are the price of admission for the life you sense you're capable of achieving. True courage lies in understanding that price, accepting it, and embracing it without hesitation.

3. The Pain of Outcome

Finally, there's the pain of the outcome—the fear that even after all the hard work, sacrifice, and struggle, things might not turn out as you hoped. This is the voice of doubt that whispers, *What if it's not worth it? What if I do all this and fail? What if the grass isn't greener on the other side?*

This fear of uncertainty often keeps us stuck. At its core, it's a longing for certainty—a desire to know that our efforts will pay off and that we'll be okay in the end. But the truth is, life doesn't come with guarantees. Sitting in certainty, doing nothing, is often the real failure. Certainty may feel safe, but it's rarely where growth happens. It's the easy way out, and that path will always anchor your growth.

Think of it like sitting in an oversized, comfortable reclining chair—a chair so soft and inviting that it cocoons you in a sense of ease. Everything you need is within reach, and there's no reason to move. But over time, this chair becomes a trap. It holds you in place, bound by invisible chains of comfort, fear, and self-doubt. It tells you to stay where it's safe, whispering, *Why risk it? Why step into the unknown?*

While comforting at first, this chair becomes a prison. It keeps you from stretching your potential, exploring new opportunities, and taking the necessary steps to grow. True freedom and fulfillment require you to stand up, step out of the comfort zone, and face the discomfort of uncertainty. A typical conversation with a client/athlete might go like this:

> **Client:** I am worried. Is everything I put in going to pay off?
> **Me:** I understand. Sometimes, we all wish we knew how things would turn out. Let me ask you, though, if I could tell you right now that you were going to lose tonight, would you not play in the game (make the presentation, meet with the client, etc.)? Would you put in less effort if you knew the outcome would not go your way?
> **Client:** Of course not! I've put so much work in, and I can't let myself down. I just wish I knew things were going to turn out okay, that it was going to be worth it in the end.
> **Me:** Sounds like you're seeking certainty about the outcome.

Client: Yes, the result. We need a win. We cannot afford to lose this [game, deal, etc.].
Me: I understand. How much control do you have over that?
Client: Almost none.
Me: What can you control?
Client: How I show up.
Me: So, what's the price you're paying for trying to control the outcome?
Client: It's exhausting me. Not knowing how things will turn out and feeling like I have no control—it's overwhelming.
(*We're wired to crave certainty, after all.*)
Me: What's a more empowering question you could ask yourself about the outcome?
Client: What *can* I control?
Me: How would you respond to that?
Client: I can focus on where I direct my energy so it doesn't deplete me.
Me: Perfect. Let's commit to doing just that!

Breaking the Cycle

Each of these pains—challenge, sacrifice, and outcome—is rooted in fear, and that fear shows up in how we approach decisions, take action, or hold back. But fear can be more than a barrier; it can also be a motivator. When we confront these pains with courage and clarity, we begin to redefine our relationship with discomfort and uncertainty.

The mindset shift begins with recognizing that pain is inevitable, but it doesn't have to be paralyzing. Growth, progress, and fulfillment lie on the other side of challenge, sacrifice, and uncertainty. The question is: are you willing to pay the price? Because in the end, avoiding these pains often leads to the greatest pain of all—the pain of regret.

So, How Do We Generate More Courage?

Stepping into courage is not one-and-done. It is not so easy to say, "I am courageous." Very much like the layers of an onion, consciously building the skill of courage requires us to peel back the layers one by one. Or, said another way, stepping into our courage means stepping out layer by layer.

Ask Better Questions

I will repeat this multiple times in this book. What is a better question we could ask? Let us start with pain and reframe this concept to the pain of regret. What pain will I suffer if I do not capitalize on this opportunity? The ability to reframe is one of the key components of high performers or high-performing people.

Comfort Zone Recognition

Recognizing where your comfort zone exists is the first step to becoming more courageous. We all have a little circle we operate under or in. I want you to visualize every one of us walking around with a big red circle around us that moves with us, almost like a holographic red circle of comfort. For some people, that circle is expansive; it extends out. It is practically intrusive on other people's circles. For others, it is so tight that it is wrapped like a belt, cinching the waistline so you can hardly see it. It is like that with comfort zones. They vary; some of them are bigger for some than others.

Be realistic about your comfort zone in several aspects: connecting with others, your dreams and ambitions, physical discipline, your mindset, self-talk, and asking for help. For instance, sharing your goals with others might be a sign of a comfort zone in vulnerability if you find it challenging. If you resist asking for help, that could be a sign of a comfort zone in the area of independence.

Expand Your Comfort Zone

Growth happens when you step beyond the familiar and stretch yourself in new and sometimes uncomfortable ways. This process can take many forms and should be tailored to your goals and aspirations. For instance, you might start by reaching out to someone who inspires or challenges you, sharing your goals with them to create a sense of accountability. Opening up to others can build your confidence and make the journey feel less isolating.

Another effective approach is to hire a coach or mentor who can provide guidance, structure, and personalized feedback. A coach can help you identify blind spots, push you beyond your perceived limits, and provide encouragement when you face setbacks. Similarly, enrolling in a program or course related to your goals can help you acquire the skills, knowledge, and mindset needed to take the next step.

You could also try learning something entirely new—whether it's a technical skill, a creative new interest, or a form of personal development. Tackling unfamiliar challenges not only broadens your abilities, but also teaches you how to embrace discomfort and adapt to change.

Finally, even small, consistent actions outside your comfort zone—like starting conversations with strangers, taking on a new responsibility at work, or saying "yes" to opportunities that intimidate you—can create a ripple effect of growth. The key is to intentionally seek out experiences that nudge you beyond what feels safe, knowing that each step expands your capacity to handle challenges and builds your confidence along the way.

Get Comfortable With Discomfort—Intentionally

A client once asked me, "What is the difference between being uncomfortable and discomfort?" I thought, *What an awesome question!* (You will soon learn that awesome is one of my favorite words.) Uncomfortable is a phrase that describes a temporary, subjective state. It is often used to convey how someone feels in a specific moment or situation. It implies an immediate experience, like feeling uneasy in a particular setting, position, or topic. For example, you might feel uncomfortable speaking in front of large crowds.

Discomfort is a term that refers more broadly to a state or sensation of unease that may or may not be tied to a specific event or moment. Discomfort can be physical, emotional, or situational, often describing a persistent or ongoing condition rather than a momentary feeling. In the context of personal growth, discomfort is the feeling that arises when we push ourselves beyond our comfort zones, when we take risks, and when we face challenges. It is a necessary part of the growth process, and learning to sit with discomfort is a key aspect of developing courage. For example, one might say that a long meeting caused physical discomfort from sitting too long. In short, being uncomfortable is a more immediate, descriptive feeling, while discomfort is a noun that often captures a general or prolonged state.

How you look at the statement above will say a lot about you. Is uncomfortability preferable because it is more temporary? Stepping out of our comfort zone requires us to be uncomfortable now and then, but if you want to build the skill of courage and to be able to tap into it more regularly, you must be willing to sit in discomfort when it comes to courage. We have all seen someone in physical discomfort and would not wish that on anyone. However, I want to refocus us on the emotional aspect of this. The second layer of courage goes from being slightly and occasionally uncomfortable to purposefully putting yourself in discomfort as it applies to growth. Let me be clear about this. No one likes discomfort, but we need to embrace discomfort to become more courageous regularly. This is where determination and resilience come into play.

Be Vulnerable

Sometimes, courage is about trusting yourself even when the path is unclear. It's the willingness to take that first step, believing that you have the tools to navigate the other side. It's about embracing the unknown, and to do that requires vulnerability. Vulnerability is one of the most vital leadership qualities. For instance, a leader who is willing to admit when they do not have all the answers, who is open about their struggles and challenges, and who is willing to take risks and make mistakes, demonstrates vulnerability. These actions can inspire trust and respect in others and create a culture of openness and innovation within a team or organization. Yet, it is also one of the most critical qualities allowing us to step into our courage. When we are vulnerable, we show who we are, which allows us to ask for help.

We must share our true goals and invite others to hold us accountable because we struggle to hold ourselves accountable, dream again, and dream bigger. We must search inside ourselves to build the life we want and to do better. Without vulnerability, we would never fully engage in our courage. Have you ever watched someone get into a pool, put their toe in, and say it was too cold to jump in and, instead, opt to take the steps one by one? They seem half involved, half avoiding, half navigating the cold water as they approach you. Now, picture yourself as the one who dives in head first. Who acclimatizes faster? The one that dives in, right? It is like that with courage. You get used to being more courageous the more often you do it. This is what the highest achievers know and do. They prioritize courage.

Prioritize Courage

The highest achievers seek opportunities to dive in and have consciously developed this as a habit. This does not mean they are fearless—quite the contrary, they have just as many fears, doubts, and worries; they do not live in **SORROW** (Sense **O**f **R**emorse, **R**egret, **O**r **W**orry). They look for opportunities to build courage. How does this show up? They share their thoughts, opinions, and ambitions more regularly. They live from a state of their strengths and focus less on their weaknesses; they invest in themselves more frequently and look at opportunities and challenges through the lens of growth. They consistently challenge and reframe their limiting beliefs, doubts, and fears. They may not always seek the unknown but are not held back from fear of the unknown.

COURAGE-COMPETENCE-CONFIDENCE LOOP

The Courage-Confidence-Competence Loop is a self-reinforcing cycle that explains how taking action leads to personal growth and increased self-belief. It consists of three key elements:

> **1. Courage – The Starting Point:** Courage is taking action despite fear, doubt, or uncertainty. It requires stepping out of your comfort zone without knowing the outcome.
>
> *Example:* Speaking up in a meeting for the first time, even if you feel nervous.

2. Competence – Gaining Skills Through Experience: When you take courageous action, you gain experience and learn new skills. Competence grows as you make mistakes, adapt, and improve.

Example: After speaking up in meetings consistently, you become better at articulating ideas.

3. Confidence – The Belief in Your Abilities: As your competence grows, you naturally develop confidence in your abilities. Confidence makes it easier to take on new challenges with less fear.

Example: You now feel comfortable speaking in meetings and even leading discussions.

The Loop Effect

Confidence fuels more courage to take bigger steps. More courageous actions lead to greater competence. Increased competence strengthens confidence, reinforcing the cycle. By continuously pushing yourself to act courageously, this loop becomes a powerful engine for personal growth and success.

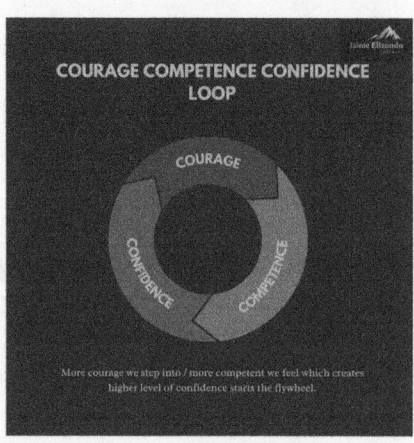

Take Consistent Action

As we discussed, action, the first step, is genuinely what courage is all about. Many people might get to this part of the book and say, "Yeah, but you do not know my situation or understand my background." You are right. I may have lived something other than your background. I may not have faced your challenges. I may not know your circumstances, but I know that you and only you can answer if you have lived your boldest self. Have you found the best version of yourself? Who did you choose to be? People often ask why I did what I did, shifting from law to football. Why did I sacrifice so much along the way? What drove me? It is easy. I always told myself I wanted to know how good I could be, so I attacked that process ruthlessly and relentlessly and broke through the barriers. My path was different, and I am still forging it. As we think about what courage looks like for us, we have to define it in a different light and in a way that fits who we want to become, not who we are.

I was blessed to have the opportunity to spend time with the New Orleans Saints and the New England Patriots, watching two of the best quarterbacks ever, Tom Brady and Drew Brees, up close and personal, and see what daily courage looks like. What I saw in them was a desire to be the best they could be. It's that simple. That is what allowed me to achieve the same.

I will paint a picture for you, whether you are a person of faith or not. Imagine that you get to the Kingdom of Heaven, and whoever is up there, the universe, God, Buddha, or whatever you believe in, says to you, *"I gave you every opportunity, but you never took it. What happened?"* You answer, "Well, yeah, I am not sure. I guess I was not as courageous as I needed to be. I could have done more. My fears held me back. I will be better next time." But there is no next time. That was it.

Let me paint you a different picture. At the end of a wonderfully fulfilled life, you get up to the Kingdom of Heaven. He says to you, "Wow, that was amazing. Do you recall when you did this? Do you remember when you were afraid, and you stepped into that doubt, when you stepped into that fear? Do you remember when you were telling yourself you could not succeed, yet you overcame and challenged your own beliefs? You doubted your doubts and believed your beliefs."

Is that not the picture we all want to have at the end of our days? So, I challenge you to live courageously.

Questions to consider:

- What does courage mean to me, and how does it show up in my life?
- When have I demonstrated courage in the past, and what specific circumstances allowed me to show that level of courage?
- Where do I need to have more courage?
- What must I start doing to look back on my life without regrets? What needs to change now?
- Who can help me with this? How can I build a team around me?

CHAPTER 2
RESILIENCE

The word "COVID-19" evokes so many different feelings. So many stories from that period exemplify true resilience. In 2020, I was coaching in the XFL, and life was great. I had a little one that was one-and-a-half years old. We were living in Tampa, Florida, in a beautiful gated community. I was coaching football and working for Marc Trestman, one of my mentors, when everything came to a screeching halt. The season was shut down. COVID-19 was taking over the world, and we did not know what to expect. On April 24th, 2020, 400 employees jumped on a league-wide call to determine the next step. Would we be furloughed? Would the season be canceled, or would we resume? There was so much uncertainty then, but we were excited to see each other after spending a few weeks at home. The most important part about football is human connection. Everybody works as a team; everybody shares a common goal.

Yet, as excited as we were to see each other on the call, we were nervous about what was next. We were told that not only was the season done, but the entire league was shutting down. Our insurance benefits would end after a week, and our next paycheck would be our last. *Wham, smack*, right in your face. That was the end of the call.

Sometimes, when we talk about resilience, we think of the times when we consciously chose to be strong or the moments when life forced us to be, when challenges hit us hard, knocking us down, and we had no choice but to get back up. A few months after that, the football world and all sports were shut down globally. There were no jobs. My wife, Aurelia, originally from Canada, was on a leave of absence at the time and not working. Together, we were raising our precious little one. With no money, no income, no job opportunities, and a great deal of uncertainty, we were forced to make a decision.

My wife had to return to Canada and cut her leave of absence short, a difficult decision dictated by circumstances beyond our control. Unfortunately, my Canadian permanent residence application was still pending, leaving us separated by bureaucratic red tape. To complicate matters further, the borders were closed, the world was shut down, and uncertainty loomed large. We had no choice but to adapt.

The only choice was for me to move to San Diego, where a possibility at Northwestern Mutual had opened up as a financial advisor, an industry completely foreign to me. As I settled into this new chapter, the reality of our situation began to hit hard. The initial excitement and anticipation of change gradually gave way to a stark realization of the challenges and uncertainties that lay ahead. Each day brought new difficulties and anxieties, and the weight of our circumstances pressed down on me with increasing intensity. The life we had so carefully begun to build was dismantled in an instant. We were thrust into a limbo that offered no clarity on how long it would last or what the future might hold. The dreams we had nurtured felt out of reach, and we were left grappling with the daunting task of piecing our lives back together in a world that no longer felt familiar. As a football family, we were used to change. As many coaches know, change and uncertainty are unwanted benefits that come with professional coaching.

So, in the face of this upheaval, we knew we had to press on and find strength in resilience and hope in the unknown. Every night when my daughter went to sleep, I would tell her, "I dreamt of you forever, and now you're finally here." I'd always wanted to have kids, so when she came into our lives, it was a dream come true. Gratitude filled my heart each evening, but alongside it came a profound fear, as our nights were counting down. She would go to Ottawa, Canada, and I would go west to San Diego. The thought of being separated across an entire continent, living in a different country, and facing the unknown weighed heavily on me. It was a mix of overwhelming love and uncertainty, both of which shaped my every thought and decision.

So in mid-June of 2020, I drove the 18 hours from Tampa, Florida, to upstate New York alone, with nothing but time to think. Rather than making the drive, my wife and daughter flew, and I would pick them up. From there, we would try to do the impossible—cross a closed border during a pandemic. I was unsure whether I would get into the country or have to leave them at the border, and I was utterly uncertain of when I would see them again. As I drove through Maryland and into Pennsylvania, my heart began racing, and a growing unease settled over me. My mind churned with anxious thoughts. *What if they separate us?* I knew there was a real chance I might not be allowed through, and the uncertainty weighed heavily on me. By the time I reached New York, my worries had only grown, my heart beating faster with every mile.

What if I never see my daughter again? The thought lingered, unsettling and persistent. *What if she falls ill and I'm not there to help? What if something happens to my wife?* The more I thought about it, the harder it became to shake the uneasy scenarios running through my mind.

What if they refuse to let me enter Canada and jeopardize my permanent resident application? The thought of everything unraveling was difficult to bear. *Who will look after her? Who will protect my family if I'm not there?* These questions circled endlessly, and with them came the nagging fear of losing everything I had worked so hard to build.

I had never experienced one before, but there, smack in the middle of Interstate 81, I was experiencing a panic attack. I was so overcome with emotion that I called my sister, Yvonne, who told me to pull over right away. Thank God I did because I nearly blacked out a few minutes later. In the back of my mind, a voice whispered, fierce and relentless: *What is wrong with you? You have faced worse before. You are resilient; you have been resilient your whole life. You are a damn football coach! Get up, dammit! Keep going!* This had never happened to me, or had it? Maybe I wasn't as resilient as I thought. But deep down inside, I knew I needed to be.

After calming down, I realized that I had also drank too much caffeine, so I began reframing my thoughts then and there. I started looking at every aspect of my life, the times I was extremely resilient, and the times I wasn't.

What was the difference? Sometimes, I was as resilient as steel under pressure, or as strong as an oak in a storm, or as unbreakable as tempered glass, while other times, I was as weak as a piece of paper trying to stop a rainstorm, or like a soap bubble popping with the slightest touch. As I got closer and closer to the border, I realized that I lacked real resilience training. More importantly, I realized that if I wanted a better second half of life, I would have to make some adjustments to learn how to develop real-time resilience, making it a strength rather than an occasional response.

The most significant insight I gained came from reflecting on the universal belief that we are inherently resilient. At first thought, it seems true—we like to think we can weather any storm. But as I delved deeper, I found myself revisiting the memories and stories of players, coaches, friends, family, and other influential figures in my life, searching for the most striking examples of resilience. What I discovered was surprising: we are often not as resilient as we believe ourselves to be.

This realization stemmed from recognizing the gap between perception and reality. People frequently overestimate their ability to endure challenges until they are faced with adversity that tests their limits. True resilience, I realized, isn't a given—it's a skill that requires cultivation, self-awareness, and practice. So why does this happen?

- The "toughness ideal" created by cultural and social narratives. We often praise strength, perseverance and resilience, which I know all about coming from the football world.
- Optimism bias. This can be positive at times, but many people assume they will be able to handle situations better than they can, like that "football coach" (me) who had to sell his house, say goodbye to his family in another country, and head to the opposite coast.
- Selective memory that overestimates our levels of resilience.

I call this "surface resilience." The two real culprits of surface resilience are when we compare ourselves to others who are more affected by stress or might come across as weaker than us and when we fear vulnerability. We all have these people in our lives. Friends and loved ones who believe they are more resilient than they are and put up a shield that protects them from feeling less or like they are lacking something or inadequate. The shield is an illusion.

I wish I could tell you everything was in check when I saw my wife and daughter. I thought I had locked it in pretty well. Emotions, check; single-minded focus (we were getting across), check; calm under pressure, check; laser-hard discipline like a soldier ready for duty, check; mental toughness, check; physical control, check; unflinching determination to hide my panic attack of two hours prior, check. But when they walked off the plane, all my feelings flooded back. My sister's voice crept back in at that moment, as only sisters can remind you lovingly, *"Duh, brother, you are moving, leaving your chosen profession to begin one that you are not excited about, and saying goodbye to your wife and daughter for who knows how long. Of course, you will feel overwhelmed and vulnerable."*

Fortunately, after a long and grueling four hours at the border, they let us through. And when I say the borders were closed, I mean *closed*. The stress and overwhelming uncertainty leading up to that moment were unlike anything I had ever experienced. The thought of not knowing when I would see my wife and daughter again haunted me as I prepared to head west to San Diego to embark on a new opportunity in an entirely unfamiliar profession. It was a situation I never wanted to relive.

For the next nine months, I lived a surreal routine of flying every six weeks through desolate airports. And when I say abandoned, I mean stretches of empty terminals in Canada that felt eerily like a scene out of *Contagion*. The silence was oppressive, broken only by the hum of overhead announcements, and the weight of the pandemic hung heavy in the air. Each trip came with its own challenges—14-day quarantines, an aching longing for normalcy, and the constant struggle to piece together what had happened to the career, family, home, and life I had spent two decades building.

I am profoundly grateful to my family, especially my sister Liz (Dora). She opened her less than 1,000-square-foot condo in San Diego to me without hesitation. Her support during that time was nothing short of lifesaving, and I cannot begin to express how much her kindness and generosity meant to me. She was my anchor in a turbulent storm, and for that, I will always be indebted to her.

From then on, when I reflected on resilience, I found myself wondering: Is it a skill, a strength, or perhaps even a talent? During the COVID-19 pandemic, this question took on a profound significance. While my own experience was challenging, it became clear that countless others faced far worse scenarios. Yet, the universal question we all had to confront—both during those initial uncertain months and in the years that followed as businesses closed and jobs disappeared—was this: *How resilient am I, really?*

Many of us learned to be more resilient; we fell, rose again, endured the challenges, adapted (I sure did), and bounced forward. But not everyone bounced forward, and not everyone rose back up. So, what is the key? What is the first step to becoming more resilient?

I have been fortunate to play a role in helping elite athletes build, develop, and grow their resilience. For years, I worked tirelessly to cultivate that same resilience within myself. Yet, in those critical moments, I found myself feeling helpless, unable to fully access the reserves of resilience I thought I had built. More importantly, I realized I had not cultivated it to the level truly required. As you've likely guessed by now, if you're going to excel—if you're going to truly "crush it" in life and in what you do every day—it's not enough to live with courage alone. Resilience is essential. It's the foundation that allows courage to thrive and sustain itself through life's toughest challenges. It's the "R" in *The CRUSH-IT Formula*.

RESILIENCE AND MENTAL TOUGHNESS

Resilience is more than just mental toughness and a grind-it-out attitude. While these are important components, there's more to resilience than that. According to the National Library of Medicine, mental toughness is a critical individual trait that enables people to handle challenges effectively and persist under pressure. It provides a psychological edge, equipping individuals to manage stress, adversity, and high-pressure situations. Mental toughness is characterized by confidence, focus, perseverance, and the ability to stay motivated even in the face of obstacles. Resilience, on the other hand, is the capacity to bounce back from setbacks, adapt to change, and maintain progress during adversity. It involves not just enduring challenges but recovering and thriving, often requiring emotional regulation, social support, and well-developed coping strategies.

While closely related, mental toughness is best understood as a component of resilience. A mentally tough person is often resilient, as their confidence and determination enable them to persist through difficulty. Conversely, resilience can help build mental toughness by fostering a sense of competence and control through overcoming hardships. The two concepts are intertwined, but resilience encompasses a broader range of skills and capacities, making mental toughness a subset of resilience rather than its defining feature.

So, what truly defines resilience? In *The Resilience Factor*, psychologists Karen Reivich and Andrew Shatté identify seven essential components: emotional regulation, impulse control, optimism, causal analysis (the ability to identify the root causes of a situation), empathy, self-efficacy, and the ability to seek and rely on support. These elements collectively form the foundation for resilience, allowing individuals to navigate and recover from life's challenges.

For myself, diving into understanding resilience began with introspection, identifying the areas in my own life where I fell short. This led me to reflect on how I had coached resilience to all of my teams and how I had personified it when we had lost a few games consecutively. Over the years, I've been privileged to work with elite athletes, top CEOs, leaders of major companies, and high achievers across various fields. A consistent pattern I've observed is that the highest performers don't leave resilience to chance—they cultivate it deliberately. While some develop resilience out of necessity, the most successful individuals have a deep understanding of their strengths and the areas where they need improvement. Ask any high achiever what makes them resilient, and they will likely give you a thoughtful explanation of the skills, experiences, and practices that have shaped their resilience. Rarely will you hear, *"I just am."*

It's a common misconception that mental toughness is enough—that simply enduring setbacks or "pushing through" life's difficulties builds resilience. In reality, resilience isn't a passive process or a default trait. It's an active skill that requires intention, reflection, and training.

With purposeful effort, resilience can evolve into an extraordinary strength, one that empowers individuals to face challenges with greater confidence, adaptability, and success.

MINDSET IS EVERYTHING

It starts with a mindset. Mindset is a fundamental driver of resilience. Mindset encompasses the attitudes, beliefs, and perceptions that shape how we interpret and respond to various life situations, including challenges, setbacks, failures, adversity, and even success. Take a moment to reflect on your mindset in different areas of your life.

- What is my mindset regarding setbacks, failure, and success?
- What is my mindset toward pressure and stress?
- What is my mindset when the game is on the line, when the deal needs to be sealed, when that presentation needs to be shared, or when that free throw shot needs to be made?

When I am on stage, I love asking how many people think they will rise to the occasion when the game is on the line. We remember the countless times Michael Jordan demanded the ball, even while double-teamed and hit that game-winning shot at the last second. We remember Kobe Bryant's Black Mamba stare-down while nailing that jumper beyond the three-point line. Time and time again, they rose to the occasion. You might think, *I will rise to the occasion, too. When I need to close that deal, I will rise to the occasion.*

I used to think the same thing until I met and visited a Navy Seal, and he shared with me something that completely changed my perspective and shifted me away from this surface resilience. "You don't rise to the occasion; rarely does anyone rise to the occasion. Instead, when the pressure is on, we fall to the level of our training." I love that. I instantly thought and asked myself, *what is the level of my resilience training? How have I purposely and intentionally developed resilience as a skill? Has my resilience developed over time simply because it had to?* That is not training.

Again, when I think of resilience, Michael Jordan comes to mind. One of his greatest quotes was, "I've never been afraid; I have been nervous, but afraid means you are not confident in your skills. I have total confidence in my skills, so I am not scared. Total confidence comes from training like no one else. He went on to share, "I've missed more than 9000 shots in my career. I've lost almost 300 games. Twenty-six times, I've been trusted to take the game-winning shot and missed. I've failed over and over and over again in my life. And that is why I succeed." Michael Jordan did not rise to the occasion; he relied on his training, extra hours in the gym, visualizing, practicing, missing, and eventually hitting the game-winning shot. His training allowed him to be great. It is the same with Kobe Bryant. There have been others, too, but these two were resilient because they fell to the level of their training, and their level of training was higher than anyone else's. Courage and resilience work hand in hand—courage to take the shot, and resilience to keep taking them when you fail.

HOW THOUGHTS DEFINE US & THE MINDSET CONTINUUM

The only thing standing in the way of success is the way we think. Let me pause for a moment and rewrite that: **The only thing standing in the way of success is how we think.**

As you read that, something likely stirred within you. For some, it rang true—a clear and resonant insight into life's challenges. For others, it may have sparked resistance, doubt, or even defensiveness. Why? Because confronting our own mindset is often the hardest part of growth. The real challenge lies not in knowing that mindset matters but in learning how to shift it. If changing the way we think was as simple as flipping a switch, everyone would do it. But the reality is, it's a process—a journey of unlearning old habits, embracing discomfort, and fostering a new way of viewing ourselves and the world around us.

Resilience, much like success, isn't something that happens overnight. Think of it as constructing a house that can withstand any storm. You need strong tools and a sturdy foundation to ensure its durability. In life, these tools are self-awareness, adaptability, and a commitment to growth. With them, you can create a mindset capable of weathering the challenges life inevitably throws your way.

Developing resilience is about intentionally equipping yourself with the mental and emotional resources to persevere. It's about building that solid foundation, hammering away at self-doubt, and reinforcing every weak spot with belief, effort, and perspective. Ultimately, shifting your mindset isn't about erasing who you are; it's about stepping into who you're meant to become. The way we think has the power to transform our lives—if we choose to harness it.

One of the best tools to help us start understanding our mindset is the Mindset Continuum. Carol Dweck pioneered the concept of a growth and fixed mindset. Through her research and in her book *Mindset*, Dweck developed the idea that people tend to have one of two mindsets regarding their abilities and intelligence:

- **Fixed mindset**: The belief that abilities, intelligence, and talents are static traits that cannot change significantly.
- **Growth mindset**: The belief that abilities and intelligence can be developed through dedication, hard work, and learning.

These ideas, though, can be traced back to Dale Carnegie's *How to Win Friends and Influence People*, which is still one of the most impressionable books ever given to me. Although he does not directly phrase it as a growth or fixed mindset, the concept shows up in his work in several ways, such as belief in personal development and the importance of developing social skills to improve oneself. Carnegie also emphasizes the power of learning from mistakes and developing a positive attitude (mindset) toward failure. He suggests constructively taking criticism and always looking for feedback on improving. The most important thing that stood out to me as a young adult when I read his book was the power of adopting a curious and open approach to others and its importance to growing relationships. What does that mean if you have a growth mindset about others? Are there only two mindsets? Do you *have* to have either a fixed or growth mindset? Does Dweck's work mean it has to be either?

While finishing my certificate in applied positive psychology, I learned about the Mindset Continuum. This concept builds on Dweck's work by introducing a more elaborate five-layer process. James Anderson expanded on this in his book *The Agile Learner*. His continuum illustrates how mindsets are not limited to fixed or growth but rather exist on a continuum or range from fixed to high growth-oriented. This allows a much more straightforward path for individuals to gradually move toward a high-growth mindset by recognizing and gaining greater insight into where they currently fall on the spectrum. This process allows others to make more intentional and realistic shifts while also bringing awareness to specific beliefs or behaviors in different areas. It will enable us to foster a lifelong learning attitude and develop greater resilience. I found that this is a great start for understanding or building an awareness around our mindset. You can have a fixed mindset in one area, and a growth mindset in another, or as is often the case, you might have a mixed mindset.

To access the Mindset Continuum Worksheet

SCAN THE QR CODE:

The mindset continuum offers an introduction and roadmap for assessing your mindset across various areas of your life—from how you approach challenges and view difficulties to your perspective on mistakes and how you handle feedback and criticism. The continuum is a starting point, but why is mindset vital to resilience?

$E = MC^2$

We've all heard of Einstein's formula for the theory of relativity: **$E=MC^2$**. While most of us may not fully grasp the intricate physics behind the equation, its core concept is surprisingly simple yet profound: energy (**E**) and mass (**M**) are interchangeable, with the speed of light squared (**C^2**) amplifying the impact of even a small amount of mass into an enormous amount of energy.

Now, let's borrow this iconic formula, reinterpret it, and give it a fresh perspective. Imagine a new equation:

Energy = Mindset × Choices²

In this context, energy isn't about physical force—it's the drive, motivation, and resilience we bring to our lives. Here, mindset represents the lens through which we view the world, influencing how we approach challenges and opportunities. Choices, meanwhile, are the actions we take as a result of that mindset. The choices squared (**Choices²**) reflect the compounding effect of confident, intentional decisions on our energy.

This little formula serves as a powerful reminder that our energy—and thus our ability to persevere and thrive—is directly linked to our mindset and choices. When we adopt a growth mindset, we approach life with curiosity, openness, and the belief that challenges are opportunities for growth. This mindset fuels better, bolder choices. And those confident choices multiply, creating a positive feedback loop of energy and drive.

Think about it: when you choose to operate from a growth mindset, you're not just making a single positive choice—you're setting the stage for a series of actions that amplify one another. Each confident choice builds momentum, reinforcing your belief in yourself and generating even more energy. This loop transforms resilience into an upward spiral, where mindset and choices feed into one another to unlock untapped potential.

So, the next time you feel your energy wavering, pause and reflect on your personal $E=MC^2$. Are you cultivating a mindset that empowers you? Are your choices multiplying your energy or depleting it? By aligning your mindset and choices, you can generate the energy you need to thrive. And, like Einstein's equation, achieve outcomes far greater than you ever imagined.

IDENTIFYING KEY AREAS TO BUILD GREATER RESILIENCE

As a mindset and performance coach with extensive experience working alongside top performers, I firmly believe that nearly any skill can be cultivated with intentional focus. The world's best hone their abilities to an exceptional level, often transforming their efforts into strengths grounded in natural talent. Among these, resilience stands out as a particularly vital strength, one that can be developed and refined through dedicated practice.

When I first began focusing on resilience, I made a common mistake: I assumed it was a singular, unified trait. Like many athletes, I lumped all aspects of resilience into one overarching concept. However, through research and experience, I discovered that resilience is multifaceted, as we discussed earlier with the seven aspects of resilience. Some of us are naturally stronger in certain aspects than others. Resilience isn't one size fits all—people face different kinds of challenges. One person might find it difficult to seek support, while another might struggle with impulse control, and yet others could have difficulties with emotional regulation. These distinct areas each necessitate personalized focus and development.

Understanding your innate resilience is crucial. Not all aspects of resilience are equally developed, and factors such as personal experiences, upbringing, social environment, and expectations can influence where we excel and where we need reinforcement. Identifying these areas allows for more targeted growth, helping to transform vulnerabilities into strengths.

> To support this process, you can access the RQ Test here. This tool can help you gain deeper insight into your resilience profile, identifying areas where you may need to focus your efforts for improvement.
> **SCAN THE QR CODE:**

MINDSET AND ONE-DEGREE SHIFTS

With a clearer understanding of the growth mindset we aim to develop and some insight into our strengths and areas for growth in resilience, we can shift our attention to mindset shifts. To simplify, resilience, as described in the resilience factor, is the ability to fall, endure challenges, get back up, adapt, and bounce forward. Simplifying this definition is essential, as resilience is deeply connected with mindset.

Earlier, I mentioned mindset is everything. Our mindset controls our view of everything. Let's expand on those earlier questions and add a few more to tap into mindset.

- What is my mindset around falling/failing?
- What is my mindset around enduring challenges?
- What is my mindset around perseverance, grit, and pushing through?
- What is my mindset around adapting and being agile?
- What is my mindset around and bouncing forward (rather than back)?

Often, lasting change comes from small, consistent adjustments—what I call *one-degree shifts or Small Turns, Big Wins*. Imagine sailing from San Diego to the Hawaiian Islands. If your course is even one degree off, you could drift far into the open ocean, far from your destination. But what if the reverse happens? What if you intentionally shifted your mindset by just one degree every day? Where might you end up? Small turns lead to big wins by emphasizing the power of consistent, incremental changes that may seem minor in the moment but compound over time to create substantial results. Like a ship adjusting its course by just one degree, these small shifts can redirect the entire journey, leading to transformative outcomes in life, work, and personal growth.

How would your life improve if you made a small, intentional shift or turn in how you approached challenges? Now take it further: imagine shifting your mindset about yourself—your potential, your dreams, or even your relationships—just one degree each day. Where could that take you in six months, a year, or even three years? I often hear, "Change is hard, coach." But change feels hard only if that's our mindset. In my one-on-one coaching, I constantly challenge this belief. The real question is, *what one-degree shift could we make today?* What small adjustment in mindset could set us on a better trajectory?

To make this actionable, we start by focusing on mindset shifts in key areas: challenges, self-belief, potential, adversity, and relationships. By narrowing the focus and committing to small, daily changes, the impact compounds over time, transforming not just where you're headed, but who you become along the way. Here are some additional questions to go deeper.

- How do I see challenge and opportunity?
- What is my perspective on obstacles and attacking difficulties?
- What lens do I see failure and my ceiling?
- What is my perspective on my ability to control my future/ownership?
- How do I take feedback and criticism?
- What is my perspective on effort and failure?
- What team have I built around me, and do I ask for help?

Purposefully developing and cultivating a focus on these areas is a starting point. Looking at what areas need a new perspective or shift helps us build resilience intentionally and not reactively.

UNDERSTANDING YOUR TRIGGERS

We all have them. Admit it. Certain things trigger us emotionally, and we often do not understand why they have such control over us or why they occur so rapidly. Sometimes, the trigger occurs before you even recognize it. Imagine that it's you on a walk in the forest; it is getting late in the day, and you are a bit lost. You have been walking for a while, enjoying the beautiful fall colors, having a moment of peace and solitude, when suddenly you hear a twig snap loudly and a bird caw out, making your heart race and muscles tense instantly. Immediately, your mind starts racing, thinking of the worst scenario: your body has kicked into fight or flight mode. It happens because our brain is wired to protect us, even if the threat is harmless.

Similarly, when we experience emotional triggers, our brain responds to certain stimuli. Whether a comment, situation, experience, or event, like hearing that twig snap, a signal is sent through the neural pathways of our brain, activating our defenses (fear, anger, sadness, or a host of other emotions) even if the danger is not absolute and exists only in our mind. However, this activation happens so fast, traveling through the nerves in our brain at a speed of up to 120 meters per second. This happens with myelinated nerve fibers. Think of them as nerve fibers with more muscle (which are coated with a fatty substance called myelin), while unmyelinated nerve fibers travel at 0.5 to 2 meters per second (which lack a myelin sheath). Why does all this matter?

Understanding what happens in our brains is crucial to reshaping it. Every time we react, the "neural pathway" is triggered and builds even more myelin around it, thus making the conduction or reaction occur even faster. This happened to one of the top CEOs with whom I worked. She could not understand why she reacted so quickly to being questioned. Shaping triggers like this is complex, but we can develop new neural pathways. Think of this like creating new rivers through the Grand Canyon. When a river is blocked and backed up, water quickly builds up, blocking the flow. This process closely resembles how our emotional triggers can swiftly hinder our progress. However, just as new rivers can be created, we can also develop new directions for our thoughts to travel, offering hope for change.

Here is how it might work step by step:

1. *The initial flow:* Recall when you did something new, like riding a bike or learning a new language. This was like the river starting to flow through an unchartered part of the canyon. The flow is initially slow, and the path could be clearer, tentative, and stronger.
2. *Repetition:* Water deepens the channel. The water flow (or electrical impulse in your brain) strengthens as you continue repeating the activity. The more you repeat the task, the more energy you give to the neural pathway. The hard part is that you are still conscious of directing the thought. Think of this as the water deepening the channel and the flow increasing.
3. *Creating new paths:* As you grow and learn, your brain does not make shallow temporary connections but continues refining and deepening the pathways. Much like the river carving intricate channels and canyons, your brain is cutting through old patterns and creating new ones (new river flows).

4. *Pathways that become rivers:* Over time and with enough reinforcement, these bureau pathways become like rivers that flow confidently through the landscape of your brain. When things begin to feel automatic, the river is in full flow, similar to how the pathway is now deeply ingrained, making the behavior second nature or a skill. This is why resiliency is a skill that can be learned. Although we apply this to emotional triggers, the same can be done with the other areas of resilience, impulse control, optimism, reaching out for help, developing belief in yourself, etc.
5. *Adaptability to new paths (flexibility and change)*: Rivers often change course when new conditions (like floods or earthquakes) appear and force them to adapt. This adaptability is also evident in our brains. The more exposure we have to new information, challenges, learning, or environments, the more we access our courage to take on these new challenges, and the more we adapt, thus building more resilience.

Our brain and, thus, our resilience are constantly evolving. Applying a growth mindset means we see our ability to reshape the terrain of our mind as in our control. *Great, coach. How do I do that? How do I begin to change in the moment that triggers that impulse, the negative thoughts, the limiting beliefs? How do I do that at the moment? How do I create the first flow?*

ABCS OF RESILIENCE

The first step is to work through a formula called the ABCs of resilience. I have shared this with so many clients. The ABCs of resilience is a simple but powerful framework for building resilience and managing adversity. Martin Seligman, a prominent author and psychologist known as the founder of **Positive Psychology**, expanded on the **ABC model of resilience** in his work on learned optimism and resilience training. While the original ABC model was developed by Albert Ellis, Seligman adapted and integrated it into his frameworks for resilience and well-being, particularly through the lens of cognitive-behavioral techniques.

The ABC model:

- "A" for Adversity: The challenging situation or event. Also, see it as an activating trigger.
- "B" for Belief: The thoughts and beliefs about said adversity.
- "C" for Consequence: The emotional and behavioral consequences of said beliefs.

Adversity can take many forms. For instance, your best friend forgetting to call you on your birthday might feel hurtful. Your initial **belief** could be, "My best friend doesn't care about me." The **consequence** of that belief might be feeling dejected and disappointed. While you can't change the adversity—your friend forgetting your birthday—you can change your beliefs. Instead of assuming neglect, you might think, "That's out of character for my best friend. I wonder if they're okay. I should reach out to them." This shift in mindset can change your emotional response and strengthen your resilience.

Another example of adversity could be receiving critical feedback about your work when you were expecting praise or a positive review. Your **belief** about the feedback shapes your response. You might initially think, "I'm a failure, not good at my job, and I'll never succeed." This belief can lead to **consequences** such as shame, discouragement, and self-doubt. You might procrastinate, avoid taking on new projects, or struggle to revise your work, creating a cycle of self-sabotage. Alternatively, you could adopt a balanced belief: "The feedback was tough, but it's an opportunity to improve and doesn't define my overall abilities." The **consequence** of this belief might be motivation, perseverance, and growth. You can embrace the feedback, make the necessary revisions with a constructive mindset, and use the experience to strengthen your skills. Over time, this leads to increased resilience and confidence.

The key to building resilience lies in the **ABC process**:

1. **Adversity or Activating Trigger**: Pause and identify the situation or challenge.
2. **Belief**: Reflect on your initial thought or interpretation of the adversity. Is it helpful or harmful?
3. **Consequence**: Recognize that your belief shapes your emotional and behavioral response. Choose a belief that promotes growth and resilience.

By intentionally challenging unhelpful beliefs and reframing them, you can navigate adversity with a constructive mindset, ultimately leading to more positive outcomes and greater emotional strength.

I started teaching the ABC model to my daughter, and let's just say it didn't take long for it to backfire. One morning, my wife came down the stairs with a look that immediately told me I was in trouble. She said, "Your daughter..." Now, let me tell you, nothing good ever follows when your wife starts a sentence with *your daughter.*

She continued, "Your daughter just told me I have a bad mindset and need to change my 'B.'" I nearly fell out of my chair, trying not to laugh, but I wasn't about to make eye contact with my wife—not in this situation.

Here's the thing I love about this (and yes, I *did* eventually make eye contact): It struck me how powerful our words and actions can be, especially when we start applying the tools we're learning. My daughter may have called out her mom's "B," but she's already grasping the concept of reframing beliefs, and isn't that the point? Even if it gets me in hot water now and then, it's a win in the long run!

FIND YOUR "YET" TO DEVELOP SELF-EFFICACY

The second tool I want to share with you is the power of "yet." When you add yet to a limiting belief or a doubt, it completely changes the dynamic. It is a simple three-letter word, but sometimes, minor things make a huge difference. So much around resilience involves enduring failures; failure is a big part of life. Fail enough at something, and it becomes a belief. If you believe something long enough, it becomes a part of your identity, and then you risk becoming a part of your core and having your subconscious make sure you are acting out this belief with your behaviors. Do you see the rabbit hole?

"Yet" changes all that. I have not spoken in front of 20,000 people *yet*. I have not mastered my thoughts *yet*. I have not [*fill in the blank with your goals or dream*] *yet*. Teaching this to our kids is crucial as it builds a considerable part of resilience and self-efficacy. The belief that we can develop ourselves, achieve our goals, and overcome challenges is vital to creating the life we envision. It plays a crucial role in our daily motivation and, more importantly, in building our emotional resilience and, ultimately, our choices and behaviors. This ability to add a three-letter word to create an entirely different mindset is potent and empowering. It allows us to shift the lens of judgment and build our self-efficacy and overall resilience more intentionally.

How do we build self-efficacy?

1. Get The *First* First Down—Generate Your Own Win

Too often, we jump out the gate with audacious goals. I am all for going big and being bold, but I believe there is a path to developing that vision. If the gap between the vision and the first step is too large, you risk losing confidence in that big, bold vision of yourself and your dreams. Small wins are those manageable, incremental successes that serve as stepping stones toward larger achievements. They act as confidence boosters, showing you that progress is possible and motivating you to keep moving forward. Each small win builds momentum, strengthens your belief in your abilities, and lays the groundwork for tackling bigger challenges. Creating small wins builds confidence. In my football career, we emphasized both first-half success and second-half success, knowing that the first half sets the tone for the game. A strong start builds momentum, instills confidence, and helps the team stay focused. That's why we dedicated significant time during the week to preparing plays that would ensure a solid opening.

A critical part of this preparation was making sure the quarterback felt comfortable with the "First 15"—the first 15 plays of the game.

These plays were carefully scripted to maximize our chances of starting strong. Ultimately, our primary goal was simple: secure the first first down of the game. That initial success was the key to setting the tempo and establishing the momentum we needed to carry us forward.

Having "first-half success" by getting the *first* first down reduced the pressure and gave everyone a psychological boost. Today, I do that by creating a morning win. My morning win comes from crushing it every morning. Ben Newman calls it his "prizefighter morning," while Robin Sharma calls it "the 5 AM Club." Whatever you do or whatever you call, it does not matter. What matters is the importance of intentionally winning the first half of your day. Mine consists of tapping into my burn, meditating, visualizing, focusing on others through gratitude, hydrating, working out, planning, and sneaking in a few minutes to read and decompress. By honoring that commitment to myself, I create the first-half win.

2. Second-Half Adjustments

The second half in football is often more important because you are closer to the outcome. So, in the second half of my day, I pause (like a game's halftime) and give myself five minutes to adjust. Have you ever known a coaching staff or a team go into the locker room at half and stare at each other, then go out and play the second half without any adjustments? Sounds ridiculous? Well, how often do we do that in our daily life? Adjusting your second half is a critical test of adaptability and allows me to build my resilience daily by intentionally making adjustments. Success from these adjustments helps remind me to be flexible and tactical, and it helps me maintain momentum as the wear and tear of the day (game) goes by. I am not saying to treat each game as a game day. That is unrealistic, but you can take principles from a game and apply them daily. Seeing consistent performance across both halves of your day is ideal. It does not always happen, but I know that no matter what the day throws at me, I have first-half success when I crush my morning routine. Doing this also helps me manage my emotional and physical well-being, and one thing I know is that self-efficacy can be undermined by fatigue, anxiety, and stress. More on that later.

3. Key Takeaways: Learning from Every Snap

In football, every snap—whether it results in a big gain or a loss of yardage—offers something to learn. The key is to keep track of the lessons, both from the wins and the setbacks. Just like reviewing game film, it's about breaking down what worked and what didn't to improve for the next play, the next quarter, or the next game. How often do you do this? Think of it like evaluating game tape weekly or even daily. Challenge yourself to identify one lesson learned each week from a success and one lesson learned from a failure. If you're aiming for championship-level improvement, try doing this daily. Remember, consistent self-review keeps you in the mindset of constant improvement, turning every success into a repeatable strategy and every failure into a stepping stone for growth. Just like in football, the more intentional you are about learning, the stronger your overall performance becomes.

4. Skill Stacking

To improve your self-efficacy, think of it like preparing for a big game. Start by creating a playbook—a list of the skills you'll need to succeed in the future—and start training for them today. Just like in football, where players practice routes, blocking schemes, and situational plays well before game day, working on these skills now ensures you're ready when the moment comes. In football, film study is a critical practice where players and coaches analyze game footage to identify strengths, weaknesses, and tendencies—both of their own team and their opponents. This disciplined review helps refine strategies, improve decision-making, and correct mistakes. Similarly, in life, we can apply this principle by regularly reflecting on our actions, choices, and experiences. By reviewing our daily "film"—whether through journaling, self-evaluation, or seeking feedback—we gain insight into our patterns, learn from our missteps, and make intentional adjustments for growth. Just as in football, consistency in this practice leads to sharper awareness and long-term success.

Often, we focus on mastering one skill at a time, which can leave us feeling like we're always playing catch-up or missing something. But just as a well-rounded football player learns to run, pass, block, and tackle, intentionally developing multiple skills at once pushes us out of our comfort zone. It builds confidence that we're capable of growing in different areas simultaneously, reinforcing our belief in our own abilities.

By approaching self-development like a football season—layering your preparation, refining your techniques, and reviewing your progress—you strengthen your self-efficacy. Each skill you develop becomes another tool in your arsenal, just like learning a new play or adjusting to different defensive schemes. The more versatile and prepared you are, the more confident you'll be when the game is on the line.

5. Eliminate The Chatter

Of all the challenges I encounter with clients, the most consistent one I encounter is the ability to block out the chatter. Regardless of our profession, the ability to take the limiting doubts and beliefs, or the noise in our head, is 100 percent dependent on us being able to talk to ourselves rather than listen to ourselves. When we listen, we go on autopilot. When we talk, we are the ones leading the orchestra. We all know the benefits of positive self-talk- increased motivation, better problem solving, more confidence and resilience, less stress, reduced negative thoughts and limiting beliefs, reinforcement of beliefs and identity, and a greater likelihood of achieving our goals. Yet, why don't we do it? I firmly believe it's our way of protecting ourselves. It's easier to avoid practicing positive self-talk than to challenge the negativity we've grown accustomed to.

But here's the truth: maintaining positive self-talk, especially at first, is hard. I like to compare it to working out. We go through phases—sometimes we're consistent, feeling great, and making progress. Other times, we lose focus, skip a few days, and eventually stop altogether. Then, inevitably, we remind ourselves how much we love the way we feel when we're consistent, and we wonder why we don't stick with it. Sound familiar? It's the same story with positive self-talk.

Many of my clients struggle with this. The key is resilience and consistency. Just like working out, you have to make it part of your routine. The more you practice, the stronger and more natural it becomes. To help you stay on track, scan the QR code for resources and strategies to improve your self-talk. Remember, the results are always worth the effort.

RESILIENCE AND OWNERSHIP

We build more resilience when we take 100 percent ownership of our life. Not 50 percent—no excuses, no blaming life circumstances, and no pointing fingers at anyone else. True progress comes from taking **100 percent ownership** of your journey. You alone control your path, your choices, and ultimately, your outcomes. For years, as I waited for an opportunity in the NFL, I did great things in football north of the border. Two Grey Cup trips in three years, one championship, six playoff appearances, and I kept saying if I just kept doing great things, someone would notice and grab me from the NFL. After a few years of waiting, I remembered a quote I was taught early on.

I was responsible for some work around the house as a kid. On one cold fall day, I was tasked with raking and bagging the fallen leaves. The leaves had gathered up, and I had completely delayed doing my shit, so to speak. I had been goofing around, knowing full well that the yard had to be cleaned, the leaves raked, put in bags, and hauled away, and like a kid, I delayed and delayed. I didn't do it. I went to sleep, and the next day, I had football practice, but the leaves were all over the place; it had rained, and my stepdad, clearly upset, said we were not going anywhere until the leaves were cleaned up. I remember asking for help, pleading that I would do it after practice, and he sat me down and said, "Son, no one is coming. No one is coming to pick these leaves up for you; no one is coming to fix things. When you screw things up or do things in the wrong way, you have to fix it. You alone." It took a lot longer than I expected, but I cleaned up those damn leaves and missed practice, which had other consequences. That stuck with me as a young boy and has stayed with me throughout my life. Mel Robbins has taken this expression and made it popular today, but for me, it was a lesson I learned years ago.

Those lessons were instilled in me early on. I remember when I was five or six, I had done something wrong. Funny enough, I can't even remember what it was. But my stepdad's punishment was clear: dig holes in the backyard, about a foot deep, and then fill them back up. I don't recall the exact lesson he was trying to teach, but for a six-year-old, it was brutally hard and unforgiving work. By today's standards, it might seem questionable, but in its own way, it reinforced a simple truth —if I messed up, it was on me to fix it or live with the consequences.

Today, as I sit with clients and drive leaders to improve at some point in our sessions, this always comes up. I tell them, look them squarely in the eye, or lower my tone if we are on a phone call and say, "[*Insert name here*], no one is coming!" Just as no one was coming to pick up the leaves in my backyard as a kid, no one is coming to fix your finances, clean up your mess, build your dreams, create the content, bring in clients, make you a better leader, elevate you to new heights, or wave a magic wand and grant you your deepest desires. There is no knight in shining armor coming to save you. For most, hearing this causes anxiety at first. It does not make them feel better. Their heart starts racing, their mind begins churning non-stop, and their palms get sweaty. However, after the first shock, they begin to feel empowered. They begin to see a blessing in that no one is coming. They are in total control of their future. When you take that level of ownership, you develop incredible resilience.

BUILDING YOUR PERSONAL DREAM TEAM: TREAT YOURSELF AS THE TEAM AND SURROUND YOURSELF FOR SUCCESS

Have you ever thought of yourself as a team? Yes, YOU are a team. The concept of "You, Inc." emerged as a metaphor for personal branding and entrepreneurial thinking applied to individuals, emphasizing that each person should manage their life and career as if they were their own company. While the exact origins are debated, the idea became widely popular in the late 1990s and early 2000s, especially with the rise of career-focused literature and the growing influence of self-help and business philosophy. It was highlighted and gained significant traction with Tom Peters' article, "The Brand Called You," published in *Fast*

Company magazine in 1997. In it, Peters argued that everyone is their own brand and should actively market and manage themselves like a company. I coach this concept by drawing parallels to the football world, where building a strong, cohesive team is essential—but in this case, *you* are the team. Who would you draft to your roster? Who would you surround yourself with to ensure success? Just as a winning football team relies on players, coaches, and support staff, we know we can't do it alone—so it's crucial to carefully choose the people who will challenge, support, and elevate you to reach your goals.

Would you talk to a team the same way you do to yourself? Would you deprive your team of the things they need? Would you always be a pessimistic head coach? Would you constantly downplay your team's successes and set low expectations for your team? "Let's see if somehow, by the miracle of God, we can win one game this year." Sounds ludicrous, right? Yet, all the things we discussed above play into the scenario above.

So, who would be on your team? Who is on it now? Who would you trade (prima donna high-maintenance players and energy vampires)? Who would you need to acquire (coach or mentor)? Ever wonder why teams are more resilient than individuals? They have a support system. They have people around them who can help handle the stress, support you when you are down, research a new area, step in, and hold your spot while you are injured. So, how do you ask for help when it comes to resilience? What team have you built, or are you still telling yourself you can do it alone, as you always have? Quit living that lie. To achieve elite levels of performance and CRUSH-IT you need to be vulnerable and courageous enough to build a group around you that will help you develop the resilience you need to achieve the huge goals.

ACCEPTING FEEDBACK

I struggled in this area. When I was younger, I always said I wanted constructive feedback, but I was too into my feelings to truly want it, much less do anything with it. I didn't like the hard stuff. Few do. The hard feedback sucks. You have to get into the right frame of mind to hear it. However, when you do, the skill of developing resilience will blossom. I learned to embrace the harsh criticism as a coach because I got a dose of the hard stuff every week. Working for Doug Marrone, the head coach at Syracuse University, where I served as the receivers coach, was no easy task, but he made me better.

Heading into a post-game meeting the day after a game, you knew without a doubt you were in for 100 percent unfiltered, relentless, no-holds-barred, fire-breathing coaching about your—or your unit's—performance. It was raw, honest, and exactly what you needed to hear. But definitely not what you wanted to hear. You were responsible for everything that your players did or did not do. It did not matter that you had covered it repeatedly during the week, that they did it correctly seven or eight times in practice, that they got it right on their test (yes, football players get tested in their preparation for the game), or that you had gone over it on the field on the play prior. It was on you! When it was your player who made the mistake, you knew IT was coming. I remember once when the offensive coordinator called a play in the red zone on the 16-yard line that was game-planned to be called from inside the 15-yard line. That one was a doozy, but I learned that Doug was driving a certain level of ownership. Whether you agreed with the style or not, the point was that the ownership is what mattered.

Developing resilience by getting consistent, tough feedback is what matters. When we embrace a growth mindset around tough feedback, we grow faster while increasing our resilience. Today, too many of us shrink away from the feedback that allows us to improve ourselves. We get into our feelings too much rather than seeing them for what they are. One client developed a great attitude around this and shifted his lens to see everything as feedback. Sometimes I have to look for it, but how much better is it when someone gives me feedback? I embrace it.

Optimism is deeply connected to resilience, as both are directly tied to mindset and our ability to shift it. When we approach life with optimism and positivity, something remarkable happens: our brains expand their capacity. Optimism engages the prefrontal cortex—the area responsible for problem-solving, creativity, and forward-thinking. In this state, we naturally begin to seek solutions and, as Ben Newman aptly puts it, "attack the process." In contrast, negativity narrows our perspective and shifts control to the amygdala, the emotional center of the brain. This often leads to reactive, emotion-driven behavior, making it harder to think clearly or adapt effectively. Building resilience, therefore, requires purpose and intention. It's about consciously choosing optimism, even in the face of challenges, and embracing the journey as an opportunity for growth and transformation.

EMBRACING THE JOURNEY

At this point, we all know that the road will have bumps and leave bruises. We all know that at some point in the journey we will get hit with a challenge and that it will be hard—be it relationships, a new career, launching a business, moving, or raising kids. Yet, we still try to control the outcome. Embracing the journey is crucial because it shifts focus from merely reaching a destination to appreciating each step. When we value the journey, we cultivate patience, resilience, and gratitude, recognizing that the small experiences, challenges, and triumphs all contribute to our growth.

One of the greatest benefits of embracing the journey is that it keeps us in the moment. In football there is an expression, "Be where your feet are." That is a good reminder to stay in the moment. When we are constantly fixated on an end goal, we often overlook the lessons and moments happening in the here and now. The journey teaches us adaptability, as it rarely goes exactly as planned, and these unexpected twists develop flexibility and strength. Additionally, embracing the journey can bring a deeper sense of fulfillment. Achievements may be fleeting, but a meaningful journey enriches our lives, filling it with memorable experiences and connections. This mindset also reduces stress and anxiety associated with reaching perfection or achieving specific milestones, as we learn to find value in the process. Early in my career, I focused on the wins and losses, getting too low when we lost and not enjoying the victories enough. I was always focused on the next game.

In 2016, we won the Grey Cup but began 2017 1–6. I was a mess. I remember before a game against the Montreal Alouettes, I was walking around several hours before the game, and I felt anxious, nervous, and uncertain, everything I coached my players not to feel. Although we won that game, I knew something had to change. I had to find a way to embrace the journey and manage the wins and losses better. As I matured in the profession, I realized that I had to find a different way to define what a win would look like. I could not keep beating myself up after every loss or I was not going to last long. Football is different from other sports and requires a different level of resilience. There are fewer games than in basketball, baseball, or hockey. That means each game carries more significance, every win weighs more, and every loss sucks the life from you. Nonetheless, I realized that no matter how good a play-caller I became, we would lose some games. I had to learn to enjoy things more—I had to embrace the journey.

In a broader sense, every journey is ongoing, even after specific goals are reached or accomplishments are earned. By embracing it, we build a mindset that serves us in all areas of life, appreciating each moment and the personal growth it brings, rather than measuring success by destination alone. That season, after a 1–6 start, we made the playoffs, winning seven of the next 10, but more importantly, I was able to appreciate the process more, I enjoyed calling plays more, and overall, I released an incredible amount of stress. I also released a tremendous weight by shifting my mindset to embrace the journey and releasing control over the outcome.

Embracing the journey does not mean we have to like the losses or setbacks. It does not encourage an "oh-well" mentality. It promotes seeing the journey and the challenges that come with it as necessary for growth and assessing the challenges as opportunities to adapt, adjust, and learn. Here are some ways I adjusted in 2017 that I have used since:

- Ask questions before you start something. *How do I want to feel after this?* By focusing on how you want to feel, you will be more cognizant of your behaviors and actions and can continue focusing on the end rather than getting caught up in setbacks or challenges.
- Set intentions when starting something new. Goals are important, but by focusing on setting intentions like "I will approach challenges with a sense of problem-solving and curiosity" or "I want to be open to learning through this process," you will be able to check and see if you remain aligned with how you want to embrace the journey and show up when difficulties arise.
- Focus on growth over the outcome or being perfect. Often, I would try to call the perfect play, and that simply was not

possible or realistic given all the variables that go into any given play. By focusing on how you could be better prepared for the various scenarios that might come up will shift your focus and allow you to focus on your development.
- Develop patience and cultivate endurance. Developing patience and cultivating a mindset of endurance, knowing that the wins will come if I continue to trust in myself and focus on developing long-term endurance.
- Embrace uncertainty and adaptability. I tapped into a skill I had used continually and applied to a larger aspect. Football is a game of adjustments, and I always prided myself on being able to make adjustments. I took this aspect and applied to my overall bigger journey in football. I knew there would be uncertainty. Would I lose a key player? Would it be a rain fest? Would we find ourselves in a situation we had not prepared for? I simply reframed what I had been doing and applied it to my career. I looked forward to the unknown and challenged myself to respond better in the moment. It became fun, another challenge that rejuvenated me. By shifting my perspective on challenges to one that is fun and almost game-like, I became excited when that challenge presented itself. One-degree mindset shifts, or "small turns," make a difference.
- Find joy. It is not always easy, but when we look for where there might be joy in a situation—sometimes you have to really search—it makes a difference. I do not mean being positive. I mean finding joy. Try this first in something you like, then when you are doing something mundane, and finally, in something you do not like. Find joy. Give yourself specific examples.

High performers do not experience fewer fears or face fewer challenges with resilience, emotional control, or impulse control than the rest of us. The difference lies in their ability to recognize these obstacles earlier and work through them quicker. A significant part of this skill comes from the mindset they have developed around these challenges.

So, where in your life do you need to embrace the journey? Where do you need to embrace the challenge? Spending time learning about resilience as a kid is not something that you really want to focus on, but it is a needed skill. Part of my mission in coaching others is simply to give them the tools that I lacked, resilience being one of them. In life, we are guaranteed only a few things. One of those is that, at some point in our life, we are going to face challenges of different magnitudes and experience struggles. We are going to be hit with some surprising moments that always come at different times and in different shapes and sizes.

Regardless of their form and intensity, we always have a choice to make. That choice is often where resilience comes in. We can either focus on the problem and let it take over our thoughts, our emotions, and our behaviors, or we can embrace the challenge and the struggle and then decide to reframe our thinking and shift our mindset. The best athletes in the world, the most successful people, the highest performers, have all built this mental muscle to maintain the right perspective when things go sideways.

Although I coached professional football for 22 years, my own football playing career ended in high school due to a surgery on my stomach. Surprisingly, this led me to pick up a tennis racket—a sport that seemed out of place for someone from a family of modest means. Yet, I excelled at it, eventually playing for the University of Maryland and even competing in small professional tournaments. Tennis became a passion, and to this day, I love watching matches because of the raw mental battles on display.

In tennis, you can see the exact moment when the pressure becomes too much for a player. I remember watching a Wimbledon final where, as the match reached a tiebreaker, you could see the stress break one player down. Their body language shifted, their focus wavered, and the strain became visible—almost like their armor was falling apart. Individual sports like tennis, golf, and gymnastics reveal these moments of vulnerability so clearly. You see players kicking the ball, throwing up their palms in frustration, or showing defeat in their posture. But just as compelling are the moments of resilience—when someone falters, struggles, and yet, finds a way to rise and keep going.

In individual sports, the challenge of quieting the mind becomes paramount. Unlike in team sports, where a breakdown can often be masked by teammates' support, encouragement, or even a shared burden, in individual sports, there's no one to lean on in the moment. It's just you, your thoughts, and your ability to overcome them. That's what makes these sports so captivating—the raw display of mental toughness, or sometimes, it's unraveling.

With individual sports, you are on your own, especially in tennis. So, your ability to develop incredible resilience in those moments is key because things will go sideways. That all stems from our ability to shift our mindset, change our beliefs, and truly doubt our doubts. The question for you is, where do you need to develop a higher level of resilience, and how can you make this a daily habit? The CRUSH-IT program is a dynamic seven-week journey designed to instill powerful habits through daily progress. By reinforcing consistency, it transforms small actions into lasting behavioral change, setting the foundation for long-term success.

To access the
CRUSH-IT Program

SCAN THE QR CODE:

The resilience tools are there, which you will be working with daily to help you develop this skill and ultimately turn it into a strength. Since courage and resilience go hand-in-hand, the more courage you have, the more resilience you will build because you will fail more. The more resilient you become, the more you are willing to be courageous and take further steps and action. Courage does not guarantee success, and neither does being resilient. They are, however, tickets into the arena. That is why they are the two first parts of the CRUSH-IT program. Courage and resilience simply allow you an open door to step into the arena. That is how you begin to go from high potential to elite performance.

You may ask yourself, why is resilience so important? Why is it the ticket into the arena, and how does it truly elevate performance? The answer lies in the connection between resilience and self-trust.

Resilience is not just about bouncing back from adversity; it's about building a foundation of confidence in ourselves. By nature, we are often more committed to not letting others down than to holding ourselves accountable. Resilience shifts that dynamic, heightening our ability to regulate emotions, live with optimism, and seek help when needed. These tools are all interconnected, and they stem from our capacity to reshape our mindset in the face of adversity—a skill directly tied to self-trust.

Self-trust begins with a habit of courage and is forged through consistent resilience. At its core, self-trust means doing what you say you will do. Research shows that one of the greatest sources of everyday anxiety is failing to follow through on our commitments to ourselves. It creates stress, doubt, and a sense of internal division. When we're not aligned with our higher selves and fail to step into the courage required to follow through, that doubt leads to delays, excuses, and further disconnection. Resilience, however, bridges this divide.

Every time we honor our commitments—whether it's sticking to a workout plan, a diet, or simply refraining from unhealthy habits—we strengthen the muscle of self-trust. We've all experienced the disappointment of letting ourselves off the hook. Think of how many diets, workout plans, or New Year's resolutions have crumbled by February 1st. The common thread isn't just a lack of discipline; it's the absence of emotional regulation and boundaries.

How many times have you told yourself, *I won't drink alcohol, eat sweets, or snack late at night,* only to find yourself reaching for that bottle, candy wrapper, or bag of chips? Resilience is built when we regulate those impulses, honor our boundaries, and refuse to let ourselves off the hook. As we do this consistently, we develop self-trust—and here's the key: the more self-trust we build, the better prepared we are to handle life's curveballs. When we trust ourselves, we develop a mindset that says, "No matter what happens, I will figure it out." That sense of self-reliance and confidence is incredibly powerful and, most importantly, is cultivated over time through purposeful action and resilience.

So, I challenge you again: What is your game plan for developing resilience?

How can you make this an intentional skill to develop? What is your level of resilience training, and what needs to be upgraded?

It took me a long time to grasp the concept that no one was coming. Somewhere along the way, I had forgotten the lesson as a young boy, or so I thought, but I realized I had not totally forgotten it. Waiting for the NFL had nothing to do with ownership; it had everything to do with unconscious programming and identity.

CHAPTER 3
UNSTOPPABLE

I had been waiting for this day for a long time. I was in my mid-20s, deep into my second year of law school, balancing coursework with an unusual side commitment. Nearly every day, I had to explain to my law school friends why my fingers were raw, covered in cuts, and looked like they had been through a meat grinder. They couldn't understand why I always showed up to class with bloody, battered hands.

What they didn't know was that in between studying cases and attending lectures, I was volunteering at the University of Maryland—my alma mater (yes, I'm a proud Terp). I spent countless hours stuffing envelopes with recruiting letters, helping send out offers to some of the top high school football players in the country. It wasn't glamorous, but I was willing to do whatever it took to be part of the game I loved.

Six months in, I was going to the football recruiting office every day. Day after day, the coaches, the support staff, and even the athletic director would see me show up diligently for three to four hours a day, stuffing envelopes.

To say that it was fun would be a lie, but I had developed the ability to grind through difficult things. Then, finally, the day had come. I was scheduled for a meeting with the assistant head coach —let us call him "Coach." I was incredibly excited and well-prepared. Coaching football was my true passion, and even though I was in my second year of completing my law degree, coaching was what I had wanted to do for years, and the opportunity to do so was on the horizon. I felt really good. Everyone had noticed and commented on my work ethic, and surely they saw me every day, in the office and on the field, helping out in any needed way. I did not take this meeting lightly. I knew how hard it was to break into football at this level, and I prepared for weeks, pouring over reports, analyzing opponents, and seeing where I could make a difference. I knew the top recruits we were going after and was prepared to discuss them. I practiced sharing my thoughts by putting myself through all the possible questions. I arrived early, calm but filled with anticipation. I told myself to convey strength, add value, and listen. I did not have to listen for long.

Rewind two years, and I had just finished my first year of law school. While I was doing well academically, I found myself questioning whether this path was truly for me. I had pursued law school with the goal of earning a professional degree, but despite my discipline and hard work, I felt unfulfilled. The days were long and monotonous, with little joy—except for Sundays or any time someone wanted to talk about football. Those moments sparked something different in me. My energy shifted, and I felt alive. (This energy shift is an important indicator I'll discuss later.) Then one day, my girlfriend, who wasn't even a football fan, casually asked me why I didn't just coach football. She pointed out that my face lit up every time I talked about it or watched a game. At first, I brushed off the idea, but her observation stuck with me. Little by little, I started to take her suggestion to heart, and it set me on a path I hadn't dared to consider before.

I took the next year off from law school, focusing on coaching and teaching, volunteering at Georgetown Prep, a high school in Bethesda, Maryland. I got my feet wet, coaching the freshman team's defense and volunteering at the University of Maryland's recruiting office. At Georgetown Prep, I could not have had a better first mentor than the head coach, Dan Paro. Many of the best football players in the NFL know the name, Dan Paro. He was a wonderful influence, and without any experience coaching football, he welcomed me, embraced me, and saw something inside me that signified I was different. Returning to the University of Maryland, on the other hand, was the opposite experience.

As I walked into that office, feeling fully prepared, excited, and ready to take the next step into coaching—whatever that step might be—the assistant head coach looked up at me and said, "You've been around here a lot lately, haven't you?"

"Yes, sir," I replied confidently.

He leaned back slightly, sizing me up. "So, you want to coach football?"

"Absolutely," I nodded, my determination evident.

He studied me for a moment and then said, "That's why you've been putting in the work these past six months?"

"Yes, sir," I confirmed, standing tall.

Then, with a slight smile, he leaned forward, his next words cutting deeper than I could have anticipated.

"That's impressive. But today, I'm going to do you a favor." For a brief second, I felt a flicker of hope. But then he dropped the hammer—the words that left an indelible mark on me and unconsciously shaped my actions for years to come.

"You'll never be more than a high school football coach."

Those words hung in the air, heavy and piercing, altering the way I approached my journey from that moment on.

Now, no disrespect to high school football coaches. In fact, high school football coaches are some of the best coaches in all of football. They set the foundation for their schools, their communities, and individuals to grow and prosper. They also do it with limited budgets and scarce resources and are often severely underpaid as teachers and coaches. Simply said, high school coaches change thousands of people's lives.

So, perhaps that university assistant coach thought he was doing me a favor. In fact, he said, because I never played professional football or played college football, I should go across the street to the athletic department. That was the right track for me. As you can imagine, I was not going to just turn and walk out, not after all the preparation and all the time. This is what I wanted, right? This is what I had been waiting for. Then it hit me right then and there, a smack in the face, all the upbringing in that moment, all that subconscious programming. I returned to the identity handed to me, the one that screamed out that I was not good enough for this, that I didn't belong there, that I should go get a job in sales (my stepdad's voice ringing in my ears), that I should be grateful for what I already had. However, if I was going to CRUSH-IT in life, I had to develop an unstoppable identity and mindset.

Identity is a tricky thing. At its core, identity is our understanding or perception of who we are, shaped by our personal traits, experiences, beliefs, values, and upbringing. It's about what makes us unique, encompassing both how we see ourselves and how others see us. While we can control the first part, we often find ourselves trying—sometimes unsuccessfully—to control the latter as well.

Identity is influenced and shaped by culture, family, environment, past trauma, relationships, and, ultimately, personal choices. In the beginning, identity isn't something we consciously choose; it is given to us by our circumstances and surroundings. However, as we grow and encounter new experiences, we gain the ability to redefine who we are, challenge old narratives, and decide what we want to become.

Identity is deeply tied to a sense of belonging, purpose, and self-understanding. It informs the choices we make, the relationships we seek, and the paths we follow. The challenge is that we often underestimate how much our initial identity—the one forged early in life—continues to influence us. Its effects can linger, subtly shaping our decisions, behaviors, and even our sense of worth long after we've outgrown the roles or beliefs it once defined.

Breaking free from the constraints of an outdated identity requires self-awareness, courage, and a willingness to let go of what no longer serves us. It's a journey of reclaiming the power to define ourselves—not by the expectations of others or the shadows of our past, but by the vision of who we want to be moving forward.

I was six months into this wonderful life, completely unaware of how little I knew, or what thoughts even were, when my father passed away. That is when my identity began to shift. Unconsciously and unwillingly, my sense of self took a new direction. My mother, born in the United States, and my father, born in Mexico like I was, lived with my older sister. We owned two large ranches in Aguascalientes, central Mexico. While vacationing with my grandparents in Juarez, an infestation broke out in our crops. We had a potato ranch and a cattle ranch, and my father—a skilled pilot—was the only one who could fly the bi-level plane needed to dust the crops. Despite the risks, he went back. Just a couple of days later, after making the long drive from Juarez to El Paso, he was back in the air, doing what needed to be done. He was up there applying pesticides, safeguarding his family, our livelihood, and his crops. Then, without warning, a storm rolled in. It was the kind of storm that changes everything.

Realizing he was in trouble but lacking the fuel to reach the nearest airport, he circled in the air, trying to drain the gas from the engines, knowing the landing would be rough. Unfortunately, it was rougher than he expected. He never landed at all. Instead, as he was coming in, fighting a powerful wind, his plane slammed into a tree. My dad didn't have a chance. He died instantly at 27 years of age. Although I was thousands of miles away, at that moment, my identity shifted in ways I could not understand, shaping my sense of belonging in ways I would only realize much later. For the next forty years, I would unknowingly live and reinforce that identity. It would show up in ways that I could not even fathom and, at times, were less than desirable.

Our identity ultimately is stored beneath the conscious surface in our subconscious programming. It shapes what we ultimately believe, especially about ourselves. For better or worse, we inevitably act in ways that align with our beliefs about ourselves. Building an unstoppable identity means creating a belief that we feel worthy, capable, and a true sense of belonging. Our identity is something that can either empower us or make us feel confined. Developing an unstoppable identity starts with examining the initial identity that was shaped for us by our upbringing, environment, and experiences. At some point, we face a choice: to continue living out that identity or to redefine it into something more aligned with who we want to become. For me, the desire to feel "good enough" emerged early in life, deeply influencing my path and shaping the decisions I would make moving forward.

REWRITING THE PLAYBOOK: OVERCOMING IDENTITY LIMITS

I was that kid that was good but not quite good enough. That feeling applied in a lot of different areas. I have never been elite in any one particular area. I always felt like I had to prove that I was good, capable, smart, tough, or resilient enough—add whatever adjective, followed by enough. However you slice it, subconscious programming shows up the most when we are under pressure, making decisions, or faced with challenges or changes. This subconscious programming influences our reactions, choices, self-talk, and beliefs, which occur in ways we may not even know are happening. It also appears in our habits, routines, and automatic responses like responding to criticism, handling relationships, or pursuing our dreams. These moments often reveal our underlying beliefs about ourselves, others and how we see "me" in the world.

We often develop mechanisms to overcome those gaps in our identity. For me, it was by grinding. Sitting in that office with that assistant head coach, all that subconscious programming took over. I lost confidence and felt unsure; for a moment, I thought he might be right; he might be making good sense and offering sound advice. Luckily, I snapped out of it and, being respectful, thanked him for his time and walked out of the office, telling myself that I would do what I had always done—work harder. I could not wait to prove him wrong. A chip on your shoulder is one of the greatest motivators.

However, I told myself another story: I was a late bloomer. I can still hear myself saying, "Oh my gosh, have you heard this song?" only for my friends to reply, "Yeah, that came out two years ago." That pattern wasn't just limited to music—I was late to everything. In elementary school, I struggled academically. My report cards were filled with D's and C's, and a B was a rare sight, let alone an A. It shifted in high school and eventually made the Dean's list in Law School but this "late bloomer" identity started to define me—not just in academics but in my perceived development. Over time, this narrative became more than just a self-perception; it was reinforced by what others thought of me. Slowly but surely, it shaped how I saw myself and how I approached challenges. It wasn't just an observation; it became a belief, one that I carried for far too long.

I began to unknowingly shift my identity by working long hours, willing myself to work harder than the next person. Or, so I thought. I never actually dealt with the underlying programming. I was "choosing" my identity, but not consciously, not intentionally, and it would have consequences. I was shaped by the belief that the only way to be good enough was to outwork everyone else. This is the lens through which I began to see life, but when I think back, this imprint had been laid out far in the past. This behavior of trying to outwork others had always been present. It was my coping mechanism. We all have them. Mine was to work hard and outwork all the others.

My dream had always been to coach in the NFL. So, when I was told at the University of Maryland that I would never be more than a high school coach, it ignited something deep within me. Those words set me on a path fueled by determination and a desire to prove others wrong and achieve what I believed was my ultimate goal. This ambition drove me throughout my career, pushing me to win a championship and driving me relentlessly in pursuit of success. However, that same path also came with challenges I didn't fully recognize at the time.

The experiences and "wiring" we accumulate throughout life have a way of influencing our actions in subtle and not-so-subtle ways. For me, those words at Maryland planted a seed that shaped how I approached my work—not just with focus and intensity, but with an almost obsessive need to prove myself. That drive wasn't inherently bad; in fact, it helped me push through adversity and seize opportunities. Yet, it also came at a cost. The wiring we carry—the stories we tell ourselves and the beliefs we internalize—has a way of showing up when we least expect it. It influences how we react to pressure, how we measure success, and even how we define our worth. For me, it meant constantly chasing validation through external achievements, tying my identity to wins and losses rather than to a deeper sense of purpose or fulfillment.

Looking back, I realize that the words spoken to me at Maryland were less about what I was capable of and more about what I believed about myself. Those beliefs became the lens through which I viewed every challenge and opportunity. It wasn't just about proving someone wrong; it was about proving to myself that I was enough. The truth is that wiring—those deep-seated beliefs—can motivate us, but it can also limit us if we're not careful. Recognizing and addressing those internal narratives is essential to truly growing, not just achieving.

THE HIDDEN GAME: HOW IDENTITY SHAPES PERFORMANCE UNDER PRESSURE

After completing my first season as offensive coordinator with the Toronto Argonauts in the CFL, I was in an unexpected situation. Years earlier, I had reached out to my friend Ron Rivera when he was the defensive coordinator with the Chicago Bears, and we had developed a strong friendship. Just a week before the end of the season, I had dinner with Ron, who was, at that time, the defensive coordinator for the San Diego Chargers, and he told me over pizza in San Diego, "I think I have a shot at the head coaching job with the Carolina Panthers, and I want to bring you with me."

Fast-forward a month. Ron had landed the job as head coach, but I did not hear anything from him or the Panthers. I was at the Senior Bowl in Mobile, Alabama, where top college prospects are evaluated for the NFL Draft. On my last night there, I received a call from Rob Chudzinski, the Panthers' offensive coordinator, who asked me to meet him at his hotel. He mentioned that Ron had said good things about me.

What was intended to be a quick catch-up turned into a six-hour-long interview, and I nailed it. As soon as I left the meeting, Ron called, no more than a minute later, and told me he wanted to bring me to Carolina. I was thrilled. This was the opportunity I had been working toward. I quickly changed my flight to head back to Toronto earlier to prepare for the next steps. There was still some uncertainty about what role I would fill—receivers coach, tight ends coach, or special teams—but I was happy to be in the conversation.

Somehow, I ended up on the same flight as the Panthers staff, with a layover in Charlotte. Ron had changed my flight, and after only two hours of sleep, I was off the plane and headed to continue my interview. A couple of hours later, I met with John Matsko, the legendary offensive line coach, and Rob Chudzinski. We started discussing tight-end play, specifically the footwork required, and how I would teach it. At that moment, I completely froze. My heart raced, my face turned red, and my mind went blank. I struggled to find the words and asked to use the restroom. After a brief break, I returned and fumbled through an inadequate answer.

At that point, I was being considered for the tight ends role, not an area of my expertise, and although I nailed the receiver portion of the interview, this moment exposed something deeper. It displayed how easily my subconscious programming could derail my performance. The pressure had triggered my insecurities, and my ability to perform under that stress collapsed. It was not about what I knew or did not know.

Instead, it was about my lack of self-belief, rooted in years of being told I did not belong. It was a strange contradiction: I had been a successful offensive coordinator in the CFL and was used to the high-pressure situations of calling plays, yet in that interview, I was a different person. I was unable to tap into the typically high confidence.

Looking back, it was clear that this moment had everything to do with the subconscious programming running inside my head. Despite my success, I still grappled with an identity that did not align with my goals. How we perform in life is always tied to how we see ourselves. Deep down, I did not believe I was worthy of an NFL job, even though that was precisely what I had been striving for.

In a surprising turn of events, I was initially offered the receivers coach position, which I was relieved about; at least I had nailed that part of the interview. But within 24 hours, the Panthers hired a more experienced coach instead. I was told that the general manager changed because a star receiver's former college coach had become available the day after my interview. My agent called it "unfortunate" but reminded me, "This has nothing to do with you." Still, I believe this situation had everything to do with the identity I was carrying and my belief in my worth.

What I have come to realize is that I was operating from an identity that did not fully align with my ambitions. My subconscious programming was not in alignment with my conscious desires. For better or worse, we will always do things in alignment with who we believe we are. We all make choices based on who we think we are, and in that moment, I did not believe I was worthy of a role in the NFL. However, that experience was a wake-up call, a lesson in how crucial it is to align our internal identity with our goals.

VALIDATION AT LAST?

Fast forward to that great Cup night in 2016. By then, my identity had shifted, but there were still elements of that subconscious programming. That night was validation that I was good enough, or at least that is what I thought and believed. I had won, we were champions, and as Greg Ellingson, one of our receivers, shared with me, "Once a champion, always a champion." I had done it! This little scrawny kid from the middle of Mexico, with all these limiting beliefs, who had been told, "You are not good enough and do not belong," finally proved all those people wrong, including the coach who had told him to go coach high school football. I felt like it was done; I belonged. I was a champion. I had shed that earlier narrative; winning had cured me of that limiting identity. I had validation. However, I could not have been more wrong.

VALIDATION COMES FROM WITHIN

Over the years, I learned that our programming lays its roots deeper than we think, whether in the boardroom or on the playing field. In both settings, belonging comes down to a sense of self-assurance, self-worth, and alignment between your identity and the role you are stepping into. On the field, it is about feeling like you are an integral part of the team's success and being able to perform under pressure. In the boardroom, it is about feeling respected and confident in contributing to the company's vision and goals.

The common thread between these examples is that you show up as your authentic, confident self when you feel like you truly belong. You make decisions, communicate effectively, and perform at your best, all while feeling like an equal player in your environment, whether on the sidelines, the locker room, or the interview room. When the subconscious programming does not align with this belief, it can hold you back from stepping into your full potential, even when you are clearly qualified.

I had been fortunate enough to share meeting rooms with legends like Tom Brady and Drew Brees, sitting in the war rooms where their intensity, confidence, and conviction were on full display. It was a masterclass in leadership and preparation, watching how they dissected defenses and approached every game with an unrelenting focus. These experiences shaped my understanding of what it takes to succeed at the highest levels. At the same time, I was helping young coordinators in the NFL refine their identities as leaders, guiding them to think strategically and see the field in new ways. I was working behind the scenes, contributing suggestions that coordinators were implementing weekly. It was rewarding to see my input make an impact on the game plans and to witness my ideas come to life on the field.

And yet, despite these incredible opportunities and accomplishments, the need to prove myself lingered. No matter how much I contributed or how close I was to the game's most elite players and strategists, I felt like I had to do more, be more, and demonstrate my value again and again. That inner voice of doubt, born from years of striving and chasing validation, wouldn't quiet down. It was as though I was in a constant battle—not with the competition, but with myself—to prove that I belonged in the same conversation as the very people I was helping succeed.

What started as a sense of belonging was replaced when I knew I belonged, by the need for validation. To a certain extent, we all need some positive reinforcement, an occasional positive word, recognition, or appreciation, but for me, it was deeper. When the need for reinforcement becomes excessive or the primary source of your self-esteem, it can become a crutch, hindering your growth and sense of self. The key to striking a balance is developing internal confidence and self-validation, knowing your worth without needing constant affirmation from others. It is about recognizing your achievements, knowing you are capable, and trusting your abilities, regardless of outside recognition. Internal validation comes from self-awareness, a deep understanding of your own thoughts, feelings, and actions, self-compassion, and a solid belief in your skills and values. It is about what you bring. Why you are unique means being able to answer the question, "What do I love about myself?" This question helps define and solidify your sense of self by encouraging self-reflection on your unique qualities, values, and strengths. It pushes you to focus on what makes you *you* and creates a deeper connection with your authentic self. By identifying and embracing these aspects, you begin to forge an identity based on self-awareness and self-acceptance, rather than external expectations or comparisons. True validation can only come from you. It is moving past the notion that who you are is not enough. To do this, you have to do some rewiring. There are three things I know:

1. I did not choose my initial programming.
Our subconscious mind accepts an idea, and it begins to execute it. Joseph Murphy's classic book, *The Power of Your Subconscious Mind*, likened our subconscious to soil, as it accepts any seed,

good or bad. Think of your thoughts as seeds. Your subconscious accepts that which is impressed on it without reasoning. Plant negative thoughts, and your subconscious mind will continue to work negatively in your subconscious. Sometimes, others in our lives think they are supporting us in cultivating the garden when what is happening is they are dumping in seeds of all kinds that we are supposed to filter in life on our own.

However, it does not work that way. Although I did not choose my programming, I had the opportunity to go back and remove the bad seeds and pull the weeds out. If you have ever pulled weeds, you know some have deep, strong roots, and it can be a battle. Snap the weed off, and it will not go away; it will just grow back, sometimes stronger. You have to dig deep to get the root out. It is the same with our initial programming. You have to dig painfully. You have to get to the beliefs deep under the surface.

2. I did not choose my programming, but I, and only I, can change it.
I am responsible for selecting and cultivating my identity. It goes back to the principle that no one is coming to save me. I have to choose what I want inside that head of mine and what thoughts I want to allow in or block out. As Murphy puts it, "Your conscious mind is like the "watchman at the gate, and its chief function is to protect your subconscious mind from false impressions." Yes, regardless of all the hurt, all the programming, the trauma that we all have (some deeper than others, especially with trauma), we have to choose who we want to become and what we want our identity to be.

This choice is often the hardest, but it is necessary to create an unstoppable identity. Your subconscious mind never stops working; it is active day and night, whether you act upon it or not. However, the first step in changing it is to be hyper-evident of what my conscious mind is saying to it. My thoughts, self-talk, and beliefs all come into play here. Keeping your mind busy with the expectation of the best, the best thoughts, and the best belief about yourself is not easy, especially if you lack awareness. Mediation is the driver of self-awareness. Ask any athlete about the key to their success, and many will say work ethic, their team, and the support around them, but the elite will say being able to control their mind and their thoughts when it matters most. That only comes from awareness. That awareness is developed through meditation, the number one driver of high performance.

3. Changing my identity requires visualization.
I cannot change my identity if I cannot visualize a difference. We used to visualize as kids. We saw ourselves as superheroes, princesses, knights, performers, musicians, mythical creatures, adventurers, wizards, sorcerers, athletes, or competitors. This was so important to our identity as it built confidence and helped us problem-solve or develop resilience as we learned how to overcome the obstacles of those characters we emulated. We had to see ourselves hitting the game-winning shot, slaying the dragon, or saving Gotham. It brought us joy and creativity and helped us dream of a bigger version of ourselves. Then, one day, we stopped. Many people quit envisioning a bigger and better self, allowing themselves to daydream of buying that beachfront house, speaking in front of thousands, leading or building a company, etc. I am not talking about daydreaming but purposeful visualization, daily.

Finding the balance between seeking validation and becoming dependent on it is all about self-awareness. It's important to acknowledge that feedback and positive reinforcement are valuable for growth and confidence, but they should complement, not replace, your internal sense of worth and capability. When you start validating yourself, learning to trust your progress, and measuring success by your standards, defining your own wins, you can enjoy the benefits of positive reinforcement without it becoming a source of dependency.

Everything is about what we believe, about ourselves, a situation, our circumstances, and most importantly, our future. We all develop what are known as iceberg beliefs, beliefs that are focused on achievement, acceptance, or control. They can be huge or several small ones, but we do not know until we dive deeper.

For me, the iceberg belief (coined by psychologists Karen Reivich and Andrew Shatté who were both influenced by Dr. Martin Seligman) was rooted in a deep need for acceptance, masked by an unrelenting pursuit of external validation. At its core, I believed I didn't belong. This belief took shape early, embedding itself in my subconscious from the time I was just six months old. Something inside me felt the constant need to prove I was worthy of being part of something. It surfaced in countless ways—when I entered kindergarten without knowing a word of English, in the Maryland Football office, and in so many moments in between. Being a late bloomer didn't help. Neither did the voices telling me to settle for less, to dream smaller, to be content with what I already had. Over time, these messages became programming, reinforcing a fixed mindset that shaped my reality. The real problem? Our subconscious absorbs these beliefs, replaying them for years until they dictate our actions. For me, this programming became fuel. It drove me forward like a train on the wrong track—unstoppable, yet misdirected. It created in me an insatiable need to achieve, to prove, to earn my place. But the question I would eventually have to ask myself was: who was I really proving it to?

THE NEED TO ACHIEVE

All of this was deeply tied to achievement—the relentless drive to be more, to rise above where I had come from. It was what pushed me to earn my law degree, what fueled my pursuit of Series 6 and 63 financial certifications, and what kept me stacking qualifications, courses, and certifications, always striving for the next milestone. In many ways, these hidden beliefs—the iceberg beliefs around achievement—served me well. They kept me moving forward, pushing limits, and proving my worth through accomplishments. But at some point, I had to stop and ask myself: *When will it ever be enough?* How many degrees, certifications, and books would it take to silence the nagging belief that I still needed more—more knowledge, more expertise, more validation?

What was missing was the belief that I was already enough. That I didn't need to hoard knowledge to prove my worth. That even if I didn't have every answer, I had the ability to figure it out. It took me far too long to realize that I already possessed the tools, skills, and resourcefulness to navigate challenges, adapt, and grow as needed. Embracing that truth was empowering. I just wish I had realized it sooner.

While I am a massive believer in growing, learning, and investing in your development, at some point, you have to ask if the very concept, the need for more knowledge and understanding, is what is holding you back. The "iceberg beliefs" concept, which suggests that deeply rooted, often hidden beliefs underlie and influence our visible behaviors and reactions. These iceberg beliefs often come from that subconscious programming.

In 2020, as I shared earlier, I found myself in San Diego, California, working at Northwestern Mutual and doing quite well. As I closed out 2020 and we shifted into 2021, I was pretty sure that continuing my football coaching career was not in my future. I was in the middle of shifting my identity. I had coached college and professional football for over 20 years. However, COVID-19 put me on a different trajectory. So, I found myself in an area focusing on coaching people and improving their lives through a different subject matter—financial planning.

As I reflected on my journey and what lay ahead, a sobering thought crossed my mind: *You're in the wrong profession.* Despite my success at the time, the days were long, grueling, and unfulfilling. I was living in a different country, three time zones away from my wife and daughter. Yet, during that challenging period, I gained profound clarity about myself: I realized that the key to transformation lies in the ability to shift my mindset, which in turn, allowed me to redefine my identity. This wasn't just about changing careers—it was about embracing the discomfort of growth and recognizing that I had the power to reinvent myself. Through this process, I discovered that one of my greatest strengths was my capacity to adapt, coupled with the resilience to chart a completely new path, even when it seemed daunting or uncertain.

The easy choice would have been to stay in my comfort zone—coaching football and becoming the quintessential high school coach, a role many believed was my destiny. But life had other plans. I vividly remember one specific Monday morning. Normally, I'm a "high energy guy"—the kind of person who leaps out of bed, ready to tackle the day with enthusiasm. I've never been one to hit the snooze button or drag my feet. But that day was different. It took everything I had to muster the energy to get out of bed. This was so unlike me. As I drove to work at 6 a.m., I felt lost, uncertain, and worn down. I decided to call my sister, even though I knew I'd be waking her up. Fortunately, she was two time zones ahead and answered. I poured my heart out, admitting, "I don't know if I can keep doing this."

Her response caught me off guard. She said, "I don't know why, but I feel like football isn't done for you. Don't give up on football."

I told her flatly, "Football is over. That chapter is closed."

But she persisted, "Just don't give up on it."

Three hours later, as if the universe had been listening, I received a phone call. On the other end of the line was an offer to become the head coach of the Edmonton Eskimos, a team in transition that would soon become the Edmonton Elks in the CFL. I was about to step into one of only 41 jobs worldwide. I remember the excitement that all the hard work had finally paid off, that here was my chance. So there I went from Tampa to Ottawa to San Diego, back to Ottawa temporarily, and then across the country to Edmonton.

About two months into the job, amidst COVID-19 restrictions, limited resources because the previous season had been canceled, and a challenging environment to coach, I remember walking around the football field with our general manager, Brock Sunderland, who remains an incredible friend. He asked me what it felt like to be a head coach. I told him that I felt just like one of the guys. It is not any different. I might have more responsibility, and I might have more decision-making ability, but I am just one of them; I am just a coach.

I failed. I failed as the head coach of the Edmonton football team, and the reasons were many. Some were my own mistakes, while others were completely beyond my control. But when I look back, the most painful truth is that I failed because I was still tethered to an old identity—the one shaped years ago in that Maryland football office. I was still that guy chasing validation, letting past wiring overshadow and control what could have been a moment of ownership, pride, and transformation. Instead of owning the identity of a leader, I kept trying to earn a seat that I already had, and that hesitation held me back.

ADOPTING A BELIEF

The first step in creating an unstoppable identity lies in identifying what you want to believe about yourself. This starts with cultivating self-awareness. Dive deep into understanding your thoughts, feelings, and actions. Reflect on the stories you tell yourself and identify the beliefs that have shaped your identity. Ask yourself: *Are these beliefs empowering me or limiting me?* Re-crafting my identity meant identifying a belief about myself that was powerful enough for me to tap into. I ask my clients and the athletes I work with what is one belief they could adopt about themselves that would enhance their confidence. Remember, what we believe will surface over and over again. Repeatedly show up when we least want it, and it will, especially regarding performance. This is how it works, why we start with a belief, and how it applies to your performance.

Let me clarify what I mean by performance. I'm referring to the quality, efficiency, and effectiveness with which we approach tasks, fulfill responsibilities, and execute our work. It reflects our ability to focus, stay consistent, give our best effort, and achieve the results we desire. However, when your belief in yourself isn't strong enough, it's like driving a powerful racing car but only pressing lightly on the gas pedal. You may have incredible skills, creativity, intelligence, and problem-solving abilities, but a lack of belief holds you back from fully accessing your potential.

When this happens, it often manifests as playing it safe, avoiding risks, or passing on opportunities. The lack of confidence prevents you from fully committing, and it creates a barrier between you and your capabilities. Without a strong belief in yourself or your actions, you're unable to tap into your full potential. As a result, your confidence falters, leaving you hesitant and cautious. This hesitation affects your execution—you may take action, but it lacks the boldness, energy, and conviction needed to truly excel.

Physically, maybe; mentally, maybe 80 percent; emotionally, less. You are not fully vested and then the outcome disappoints you. The next step is the most dangerous because your failure or shortcoming is seen as a "people problem." The "people problem" is you. So you fall back into your subconscious programming. You should be grateful you had a chance to compete, thankful you made it to the Olympics, that you have a job, yet we feel shitty. It is not a people problem—it is a process problem. You have not rewired your programming. Your process starts by adopting a belief about yourself that makes you more confident. That is Step 1.

SHAPING UNSTOPPABLE IDENTITY AND MINDSET THROUGH CHOICES

Step 2: Choose better. Make choices that support your belief about yourself by making choices that allow you to tap into your strengths and access all of you. Our choices shape our habits, and our habits shape our identity. When you consistently choose actions that align with your beliefs and values, you build momentum toward becoming the person you want to be. Each small, intentional choice creates a ripple effect, strengthening your self-trust and confidence over time. Imagine how different your life could look if, before every decision, you asked yourself one simple question: *Will this choice make me feel more confident about the person I want to become?* That one moment of reflection has the power to reshape your actions, redirect your path, and ultimately redefine who you are.

DEVELOPING, MANAGING, AND NURTURING CONFIDENCE

Have you ever met someone with an unstoppable identity who lacked confidence? Nope. Neither have I. At this point, you may wonder, what does an unstoppable identity look like anyway? Someone with an unstoppable identity exudes a unique blend of confidence, resilience, and purpose that shines through in their demeanor and actions. They carry themselves with a grounded sense of self-assurance, making decisions with clarity and conviction. There is an unmistakable energy to them—whether calm or dynamic, it is magnetic, showing their inner alignment and commitment to their goals and values. This deeper level of confidence is powerful, unique, and important.

The best definition of confidence I found was in the book *The Confi-*

dent Mind by Nate Zinsser, where he describes confidence as "a certainty about your ability that bypasses conscious thought and leads to unconscious execution." In working with athletes, you must help them develop and manage their confidence intentionally. When a player drops a ball in a key moment of the game, although usually tied to subconscious programming, poor programming presents itself the most when the stakes are high. In developing receivers early on in my career, we spoke a lot about managing our confidence after a big drop. If you have ever played sports, it happens all the time: a receiver gets the drops, a baseball player goes into a slump, or you freeze up moments before your ice routine at the Olympics.

It happens to all of us. The key is what we do to manage and replenish our confidence. The problem is that very few people see confidence as something to actively manage. We often either have it or do not. Sometimes we have it because of the work we put in or the validation we get from others. But if we measure confidence through the lens of unconscious execution, it can be cultivated. So, what do you do when your confidence suffers? How do you take care of, rebuild, and reinforce it?

YOUR CONFIDENCE FORMULA

Write a checklist. This is what brings me confidence. When I do these things, I build my confidence. Basic, yes, effective even more so. This means having a personal blueprint that you can use to access confidence when facing new stressors or even when you lose a bit of confidence. The formula should include specific actions, thoughts, habits, routines, or mindsets that make you feel solid, capable, and self-assured. With athletes, it often means remembering the three best moments of their career and reliving those before a game, or it might mean listening to a certain playlist that generates certain feelings they want to have. What goes on in the first part of your formula? How do I tap into it, grow it, and nurture it?

For others, a confidence formula might mean practicing positive self-talk after tough criticism, focusing on past successes when struggling with a project, or visualizing success and how awesome you are going to feel when you complete it. The confidence formula is unique to you. It is your confidence DNA. No one formula works for everyone, yet, you need one because life will affect your confidence.

CULTIVATING CONFIDENCE

Confidence is a funny thing. We all want more of it; in fact, the world's largest leadership study on what drives high performance found that confidence was one of three things people wanted more of. Yet, how do you, specifically, cultivate it? Most high performers tell me, "Well, I set small and achievable goals, embrace growth, practice, make sure I am prepared, and surround myself with positive people." Awesome! All good things. However, cultivating a fertile ground for daily growth means constantly monitoring our self-talk until what we say to ourselves has become unconscious execution.

LIVING FROM YOUR STRENGTHS AND MEMORIES

When we live from our strengths and embrace the unique gifts we've been blessed with, we begin to step into a more powerful and purposeful identity. This process happens in two key ways: first, by acknowledging and deeply understanding our strengths, and second, by intentionally shaping our mindset through the power of our thoughts. Our self-perception is often a direct reflection of our self-talk and the questions we ask ourselves daily.

Consider the difference between disempowering questions like, *Why does this always happen to me? Why can't I get this right? Why am I such a klutz?* and empowering ones, like *What can I learn from this? How can I improve? What strengths can I leverage to overcome this?* The questions we ask shape the narrative in our minds, which directly impacts how we see ourselves and the potential we believe we have.

When we ask disempowering questions, we unintentionally limit the vision of who we are and what we're capable of. Negative self-talk erodes confidence, narrows our identity, and keeps us from stepping into the fullness of our abilities. Conversely, when we focus on empowering questions and positive self-talk, we open the door to growth, resilience, and a stronger connection with our true potential.

Believing in who we are is the foundation for living from our strengths. Without that belief, we can't fully access or utilize the gifts we've been given. We end up playing small, held back by doubt and fear. But when we intentionally align our thoughts with our strengths and commit to seeing ourselves in a positive, empowering light, we unlock the ability to live boldly, authentically, and in alignment with our highest potential. This shift allows us to fully step into the identity we were meant to embrace.

EMBRACING WHO YOU ARE

Embrace all of who you are. It's a powerful yet challenging statement—embracing not just the good but also the bad, the hidden beliefs, and the limiting thoughts we often try to ignore. When we start to accept all aspects of ourselves, including our strengths, talents, and skills, we open the door to building a super powerful and unstoppable identity. Stepping into the highest vision of ourselves is something we've all experienced at some point in our lives—those moments when we felt truly unstoppable. But the key lies in embracing every part of who we are, even the parts that make us uncomfortable, and asking ourselves, *Where does my mindset need to shift?* It's in these moments of reflection that we begin to uncover the questions that challenge our old beliefs and patterns.

A great example of this comes from the movie *I, Robot*, where Will Smith's character, Detective Spooner, interacts with a hologram of Dr. Lanning. At one point, the hologram tells him, *"That is not the right question."* This is such profound insight. It reminds us to ask ourselves the right questions—questions about our deeply ingrained beliefs, our subconscious 'iceberg' thoughts, and the identities we've accepted but may need to shift.

When we begin to ask these deeper questions, we can start to make the mindset shifts necessary to fully step into the best version of ourselves. The more we cling to an old identity, the more doubt creeps in. That doubt creates hesitation, which delays action. And the longer we delay action, the more we feel an internal divide—a sense of being out of alignment with who we truly are. To move forward, we must summon the courage to confront these doubts, shift our beliefs, and align ourselves with our higher potential. Only then can we truly step into the person we're meant to become.

VISUALIZING IS THE KEY

From an early age, I realized the power of seeing myself succeed. As kids, we did this naturally. We imagined ourselves as superheroes, athletes, or artists, creating vivid mental pictures of who we wanted to be. Those moments of daydreaming gave us confidence and direction. Visualization carried me to certain levels of success, but to develop an unstoppable identity, you need more than just fleeting visions—you need a clear, vivid image of your future self.

This is where "I AM" statements come in. Rooted in both biblical origins and popularized by personal growth authors like Neville Goddard, these affirmations help shape self-identity and manifest change. Phrases like "I AM strong," "I AM focused," or "I AM capable" bridge the gap between who we are now and who we want to become. They work because they guide us to embody the qualities we desire while reinforcing belief in our potential. The key to "I AM" statements isn't just saying the words—it's truly visualizing yourself living them out. Picture yourself as the person you want to be. With consistent practice, these affirmations start to influence your thoughts, actions, and behaviors. Over time, they become second nature, leading to unconscious execution and unmatched confidence.

Now, here's your challenge: What part of your identity needs a closer look? What beliefs have you been holding onto that no longer serve you? What shifts in mindset do you need to make to fully step into the highest version of yourself? To help you get started, I've included two worksheets to guide you through crafting your own "I AM" statements. Remember, each of us has the power to become truly unstoppable—it begins with a clear vision and the commitment to embody it every day.

Let's quickly recap: to truly *CRUSH-IT* in life, we have discussed three foundational pillars—**Courage**, **Resilience**, and becoming **Unstoppable**. These are the pillars of greatness, the fuel for living a life that's not just successful but truly fulfilling. Sounds simple, right? But here's the truth: building and sustaining this kind of momentum requires more than just good intentions. It demands energy—physical, mental, and emotional—to consistently show up as your best self. Think about it: how you show up dictates everything. Your energy influences the way you tackle challenges, the way you connect with others, and ultimately, the way you create and manifest the life you desire. Without the right energy, even the best strategies fall flat. Courage becomes hesitation. Resilience turns into exhaustion. And that unstoppable identity? It feels out of reach.

This next chapter is all about unlocking that energy—recharging your body, rewiring your mindset, and aligning your actions so you can show up with unwavering focus, drive, and determination. Because let's face it: success doesn't happen by accident. It's created by those who choose to bring their *best* every single day. Whether it's the physical energy to power through long days, the mental clarity to make bold decisions, or the emotional stamina to stay grounded in the face of adversity, energy is the foundation that supports every step of your journey. The good news? It's something you can cultivate and build, starting right now.

So, as we dive in, I want you to reflect on this:

- What kind of energy are you bringing to your life right now?
- And what would it look like if you leveled it up?

By the end of this next chapter, you'll not only have the tools to unlock your full potential but also the energy to truly embody the unstoppable identity you're striving for.

Let's get started—because how you show up changes everything.

CHAPTER 4
SHOW UP

Drew Brees stands around 5 feet 11 inches tall, but he is much larger in life than that. For those who do not know, Drew Brees is one of the best quarterbacks to ever have played in the NFL. And he did it as an undersized player, meaning he did not fit the profile for a typical or prototypical quarterback in the NFL, typically around 6 feet 4 inches and 225 pounds. I met Drew Brees when I was doing my NFL minority internship with the New Orleans Saints in 2007.

What immediately stood out to me about Drew was his presence. Whenever he showed up, the energy changed. When we are really showing up, all of us, fully present, engaged in the moment, incredible things can happen. I remember the first thing I noticed about Drew was his level of intensity, but not just on the football field. Drew had an unbelievable gift that most great leaders have: the ability to make you feel terrific, like you were the most important person in the world. It did not matter if Drew was talking to the cafeteria lady, to me, a minority guest coach, or if he was talking to the gentleman who picked up the trash. He treated everyone with enthusiasm and class.

When Drew was talking to you, you were the most important thing in the world—at least he made you feel that way. It all starts with our energy. Energy is the hidden gem of high performers, and when you operate with a certain energy level, you bring a tremendous amount of positivity. In working with one-on-one clients, and I'm blessed to work with high performers all across the globe, from Australia and Japan to Brazil to Britain to Canada, the U.S., and several others, I always start these one-on-one coaching sessions by asking what was awesome this week.

∽

We will not move into the coaching session until my clients find something great that week. Many of them know that being a high performer involves many challenges, problems, and stress, and many people I work with want to dive right into fixing the problems. Understood. Time is limited. We have things that we want to fix.

However, in every session where I have not started with what was awesome, the insights and transformation just do not appear. Research shows that when we start with a prompt like, "What was great this week? What was awesome? What has been good in your life? Tell me what you loved about this weekend," we create that positive focus that opens up our brains. We become broadened. We start using the prefrontal cortex of our brain, which is the area that is responsible for problem-solving and creativity, and when we become broadened, those two things happen. We start focusing on the solution.

We started focusing on the good things. We start engaging that creative aspect that will help us solve those problems. So, as we broaden and we have to think about what is great right now, even when we do not feel like anything is great, we are letting science and our brains take over. When we embrace a broader perspective and approach situations with curiosity, research shows that curiosity fosters greater connection. Drew Brees was the master of this. He would say that he is curious about what is going on in your life. He would ask questions about you and showed up authentically curious. So, when you walked away with a conversation with Drew, you felt like the most important person in the world.

Unfortunately, the opposite also happens. When we focus on the negative instead of the positive, our brains become narrowed. We develop tunnel vision, like looking through a microscope, as opposed to looking through a telescope, and when we become narrowed, we start operating from a different area of our brain, our amygdala, the emotional center of our brain. Our emotions are hijacking us, and we cannot seem to get out of it because we have become so focused and narrowed on whatever is affecting us at that moment.

The "S" in CRUSH-IT stands for **Show Up**, and it plays a pivotal role in how we approach life. Often, it's the key factor that determines our ability to connect, earn promotions, achieve advancement, and, most importantly, perform at our best. Showing up goes beyond just being physically present—it encompasses multiple dimensions, including energy, engagement, presence, and authenticity. Each of these elements contributes to how effectively we show up in various aspects of our lives.

In the sections ahead, we'll delve into each of these components, with a strong emphasis on Energy, as it serves as the foundation for all the others. When we bring the right energy to the table, it amplifies our engagement, deepens our presence, and enhances our authenticity. Let's explore what it truly means to *show up*.

BRINGING THE JUICE

In football, for years, we used the phrase "bring the juice." I did not come up with it, but it is a saying I have shared with the players and coaches I have had the privilege to work with. "Bring the juice" is all about bringing energy—bringing all of you and not waiting for someone else to bring it. We often find ourselves reflecting on an important question: what kind of energy are we bringing to the table? If there's one key takeaway from this book, let it be this: energy drives everything. Consider this for a moment—even when we think we need more time, what we're truly yearning for is more energy. Time, after all, is fixed; we all have the same 86,400 seconds in a day. It's not about having *more time*—it's about having the vitality and focus to make the most of the time we already have.

Productivity doesn't stem from an abundance of hours; it flows from the energy we bring to those hours. Our ability to generate and replenish energy is the foundation of everything we do, from tackling our goals to maintaining relationships and thriving in our personal lives. So, ask yourself: *Am I bringing the juice?*

Energy isn't just one-dimensional. It comes in many forms—physical energy, mental energy, emotional energy, and even spiritual energy. Each type plays a role in shaping how we show up, how we engage with the world, and how we overcome challenges. By understanding and cultivating these different types of energy, we empower ourselves to lead more productive, fulfilling, and vibrant lives.

YOU NEED FULL ENGAGEMENT

When I ask, "What kind of energy are you bringing?" it raises another question: What do we mean by *kind of energy*? Many people think of energy as that high-energy, enthusiastic person on stage. However, there are different types of energy that we need to understand and master, along with their dynamic interactions. In *The Power of Full Engagement* by Jim Loehr and Tony Schwartz, four types of energy are highlighted. There is mental energy related to focus, intellectual engagement, problem-solving, and concentration. Emotional energy involves creating positive emotions and connecting meaningfully with others. Physical energy is all about how refreshed you wake up; it is about vibrancy. Does that initial energy carry you through the day, or do you need a nap? It has been scientifically proven that some of the best, highest-performing people take power naps; more on that later. Do you need a nap, or run out of steam in the second half of the day?

The last area is your spiritual energy, which is all about connecting to something higher than yourself. For some, it means their faith; for others, it means something different. This has nothing to do with faith (although it might for some people) but everything to do with being connected to something higher than yourself. Managing these different types of energy is an important aspect of enabling us to show up as the best version of ourselves. We will break down energy management into three aspects: generating energy and replenishing it, identifying "energy drains," and transforming energy.

ENERGY MANAGEMENT

PART I: Generating Energy

If I asked you a very simple, straightforward question, how confident would you be in your ability to answer it completely with clarity, certainty, and conviction? It depends on the question, right? How do you generate energy?

> **Me:** How do you generate energy?
> **Client:** What do you mean?
> **Me:** How do you generate the energy you want consistently, daily, over long stretches of time?
> **Client:** Well...um, I work out, eat right, get plenty of sleep.
> **Me:** Great, those are all important things for helping you generate energy. What else do you do?
> **Client:** I am not sure I understand the question.

Very few of us are ever taught how to consistently generate and replenish the energy needed to show up with an unstoppable identity, day after day, over long periods of time. Sure, many of us know what it feels like to have energy, but we often find ourselves wishing we had more. We think of energy as something that comes from external sources, something we hope to have more of, but we rarely consider the intentional processes for cultivating it.

The Basics Aren't Enough

When it comes to generating energy, most of us focus on the basics: exercise, diet, and sleep. These are undoubtedly essential, and if you need guidance in these areas, I can point you toward outstanding resources. But these basics are just the tip of the iceberg. There are countless other factors that influence how we generate, manage, and replenish energy. Think of energy sources like solar panels, wind turbines, hydroelectric dams, or ocean waves. These sources don't just *contain* energy; they actively generate it, renew it, and store it. Much like these systems, we are also designed to generate energy. The key is identifying and tapping into our own unique energy sources to create connections, fuel deeper engagement, and maintain high levels of performance.

Let's start by asking ourselves a few key questions to uncover what truly fuels us:

- What activities make me feel most energized?
- When do I feel "in the zone?"
- What part of the day do I feel most alert and focused?
- Who are the people that make me feel more energized or uplifted after interacting with them?
- What passion, interests, or things do I feel a deep excitement about?
- What do I get excited talking about?
- What positive and growth-oriented thoughts can I focus on today to enhance my mental clarity and reduce stress?
- What physical activities genuinely bring me joy and motivation, and how can I integrate them?

These questions don't just help us generate energy—they guide us in discovering ways to replenish it when it's depleted. Replenishment is crucial because energy is not infinite; we must learn to recharge in ways that are both intentional and sustainable.

Why Energy is the Foundation

Being able to tap into how we generate the energy we need is crucial to understanding how to manage our energy and thrive. It is a huge part of accomplishing our goals, reaching for new levels, and elevating ourselves to discover our truest and highest potential, and once we get there, energy is what sustains us, enabling us to continue growing and thriving. Without energy, even the best plans and intentions fall flat.

Take a look at these statements:

- "I wish I had more energy."
- "I am exhausted—I need a vacation!"
- "You do not understand. I do not have time to [fill in the blank]."
- "If only I had the energy to work out."

These statements reflect a common reality: when energy is lacking, everything feels harder. Yet, we encounter those rare individuals who seem to operate on a completely different level.

The Ripple Effect of Energy

You know the people I'm talking about—they walk into a room and transform it. Their energy is contagious, lifting the spirit and motivation of those around them. This isn't about hype or superficial enthusiasm; it's about a steady, grounded energy that inspires others to rise to the occasion. These individuals:

- Motivate us to tackle challenges.
- Inspire us to elevate our own performance.
- Spark a sense of optimism, possibility, and excitement.

They bounce back from setbacks with resilience, maintaining intentional focus and a belief in what's possible. Their energy creates a ripple effect, empowering others to show up as their best selves. They don't just engage with others—they *ignite* them. When these people interact, they cultivate an environment of trust, collaboration, and shared purpose. Their energy reminds others of the power of connection, the importance of supporting one another, and the potential for growth when we work together. The result? A tidal wave of positivity, engagement, and forward momentum that benefits everyone involved.

Learning to Generate and Replenish Energy

Becoming that person—the one who vibrates at a higher level—starts with understanding how to generate and replenish your energy consistently. This means going beyond the basics and cultivating habits, relationships, thoughts, and activities that fuel you on every level: physically, mentally, emotionally, and spiritually. When you master this, you'll not only transform your own life but also create a ripple effect that uplifts and energizes those around you. That's the power of energy —it's not just about what it allows you to do; it's about the impact it has on the world around you.

PART II: Escaping the Energy Traps

To manage your energy, you need to be hyper-aware of what drains you. As we go through life, there are things that we go through daily that drain us and sap our energy. Sometimes, it's conversations or people we have conversations with. Other times, it's our job. We are all usually aware of those big energy vampires and energy vacuums. If you are not, I recommend using this checklist to answer some questions to help you identify the big energy drains in your life.

Access the Energy Drain Checklist here.

SCAN THE QR CODE:

Jim Loeher, in his book *Full Engagement*, has a terrific energy management grid that he uses to describe four different types of energy: high energy, low energy, positive energy, and negative energy. In each quadrant, he has emotions that each state generates. This grid is a valuable tool for understanding our energy. I've found it helpful to not only identify the type of energy I have, but also to track how much time I spend in each quadrant over different periods and what causes me to shift from one to another.

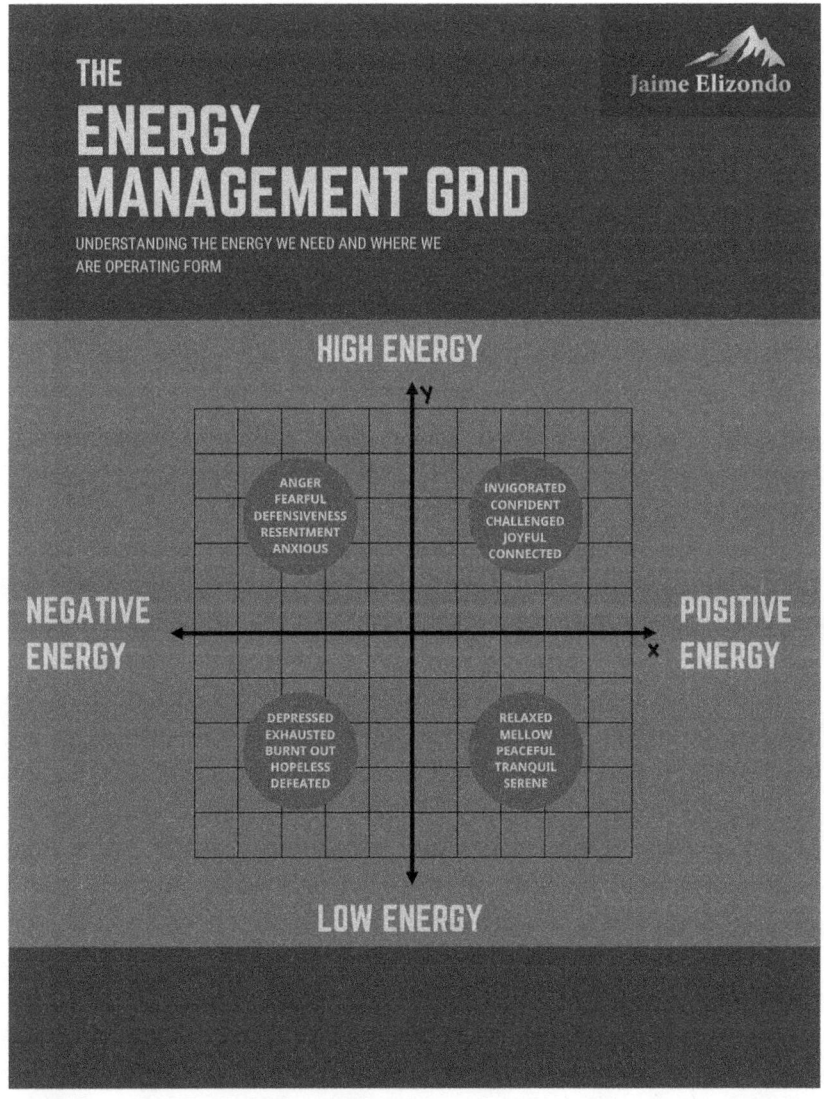

We cannot always be in the upper right quadrant, but we can be conscious of how we want to balance that energy distribution and thus manage it better. I also used this energy management grid and took a 360-degree view of the events or interactions with people, which caused me to be in one section more than the other. It is also a great way to manage your energy throughout the day and consciously control how you want to show up. Although people, events, or aspects of our lives drain our energy, there are other, more subtle energy drains—or what I call energy bleeding.

This type of loss is gradual and often goes unnoticed, but over time, it can become a significant problem. Energy bleeding comes from unnoticed sources like toxic relationships, distractions, or poor boundaries, slowly testing your strength, vitality, and resilience. Just like a physical wound, the loss might seem minor at first—a slight sting you can ignore—but as the bleeding continues, your strength begins to fade. Similarly, energy bleeding sneaks up on you. Initially, you might blame your fatigue or lack of focus on something minor, but unchecked, these leaks can have a cumulative effect, leaving you running on empty. Recognizing and addressing these drains is essential to preserving your energy and staying at your best.

Have you ever felt inexplicably drained, wondering why you're so tired despite getting enough sleep or doing everything "right?" Energy bleeding can be triggered by small, subtle sources—a negative thought, an unresolved worry, or an environment that wears you down over time. These drains accumulate gradually, leaving you feeling fatigued, unmotivated, or depleted. If left unchecked, they can lead to exhaustion, much like prolonged physical blood loss causes weakness. The key is to identify these hidden sources early, addressing them before they escalate. By becoming aware of what drains your energy and taking proactive steps to protect it, you can restore your strength and vitality, allowing you to show up as your best, most whole self.

One hidden source of energy bleeding that often goes unnoticed is transitions. Transitions—whether between tasks, environments, or life stages—can be significant drains on our energy, requiring us to adjust our focus, mindset, and physical presence. Transitions drain us; they utilize our energy. Transitions require us to adjust our focus, mindset, and often our physical presence, all of which can consume significant mental and emotional energy. These shifts may seem minor, but they consume mental and emotional resources in ways we don't always recognize. For example, think about the cognitive load required when moving from one task to another. Have you ever walked into a meeting struggling to recall the points you planned to address earlier, your mind still bouncing between the last task and the current one? This constant juggling of focus and attention can leave you feeling mentally and physically drained. Here's why transitions play such a key role in energy loss.

The second way transitions drain us is through increased decision-making. Every time we shift priorities—whether it's responding to someone walking into your office, pausing one task to start another, or deciding what to focus on next—we engage in a series of tiny micro-decisions. These seemingly minor choices, such as "What should I do next?" or "Where was I before this interruption?" add up, creating cumulative mental strain. This constant need to reassess, refocus, and recalibrate depletes our cognitive resources, drawing from the same energy reserve we rely on for more significant decisions and tasks. Over time, these small but frequent withdrawals from our daily energy account can leave us feeling overwhelmed and mentally fatigued, further reducing our ability to focus and perform at our best.

The third way transitions drain us is through the emotional toll they take. Each transition often comes with its own emotional weight. We might feel a range of emotions, from excitement or anticipation to anxiety, frustration, or even guilt. For example, rushing from one interaction to the next might leave us feeling overwhelmed, or realizing we were not fully present in a prior engagement might trigger regret or the need to apologize. These emotional adjustments, no matter how subtle, require energy as we mentally and emotionally adapt to the change. Over time, this constant emotional recalibration adds up, depleting our reserves and leaving us less equipped to handle subsequent transitions with clarity and focus.

Managing Your Transitions

Set a buffer zone. Two things I work with my clients on in this area are to give yourself a buffer from one thing to another, whether it is back-to-back meetings or going from your car into your house, to do a mini-decompression. Literally, finish and close out what you were doing before moving forward. Allow for transition time.

In the football world, we always paid close attention to the distance between the locker room and the field. That "walk" was more than just a physical transition—it was a critical moment between delivering the final locker room message and unleashing the players' energy on the field. It provided a brief yet essential window for players and coaches to focus their thoughts, visualize their performance, and enter the final stage of mental preparation. I always wanted to know exactly how long that walk would take or how much time we'd spend waiting in the tunnel because it mattered. It was the bridge between the high energy of the locker room and the intense focus needed on the field. Get hyped up too early, and you risk losing both energy and focus before the game even begins. The timing of that transition was key—it ensured the team was mentally and physically ready to perform at their peak when it mattered most.

Be intentional about how you want your next interaction to unfold. Whether we were up or down, halftime was the first time since leaving the locker room that everyone was together again. We had a deliberate process for halftime: players were given space to vent their frustrations if we were losing or to refocus if we were ahead. During this time, the coaches huddled briefly to discuss adjustments. Before addressing the players again, I always took a moment to reflect on the upcoming interaction. What message did I want to convey? How did I want to convey it? Confidence was key, but so was honesty—players, like most people, can spot inauthenticity a mile away. I always took a direct, no-nonsense approach. I asked myself: *What energy do I want to bring? What's the message, and how does it need to come across?* Words matter, but so does body language. Both should be chosen wisely.

To guide this process, I focused on my three "interaction words" —specific words that clarified how I wanted to show up for others. By grounding myself in these words, I refocused my mind and ensured I was bringing the energy and presence I needed for the next "thing." This intentionality not only helped me connect with the team but also set the tone for how we moved forward together. How many times have you walked into your home, but your mind is still at work, and three minutes go by before you really "notice" your kids? Or you go from one meeting to another without a pause, and it takes you 10 minutes to truly catch on to what is being said. Transitions drain us because they either take up additional energy reserves, or we show up less than what we want and then beat ourselves up for doing it again. Almost every client I work with at or near the top of their goals is to be more present. This is an area in which everyone struggles. There are three additional things to help in dealing with transitions:

- Batch "like things" together so you limit the number of transitions.
- Limit decisions intentionally or set aside time to make them. Block time for decision-making. Where possible, create decision-making time.
- Practice mindfulness. Awareness of your feelings helps anchor you during transitions, thus reducing energy loss.

In today's fast-paced, hyper-connected world, distractions are everywhere. From constant notifications on our devices to the never-ending stream of information and demands on our time, we are pulled in multiple directions at once. These distractions may seem small in the moment, but they add up, creating significant drains on our mental and emotional energy. Each time we lose focus and redirect our attention, we're expending energy—whether it's responding to an unnecessary email, jumping between tasks, or endlessly scrolling through social media. The digital world is designed to capture and hold our attention, pulling us into endless cycles of pings, alerts, and dopamine-driven scrolls. This constant bombardment of distractions doesn't just steal our focus; it drains our energy in subtle yet significant ways.

Distractions don't just disrupt our focus; they are a major contributor to energy bleeding. Like a slow leak, distractions siphon away our vitality without us even realizing it, leaving us feeling mentally foggy, emotionally drained, and physically tired. They chip away at our ability to be fully present and engaged, impacting our productivity, relationships, and overall sense of well-being. Recognizing the role of distractions in energy bleeding is the first step toward minimizing their impact and preserving the energy we need to thrive.

Research suggests it takes 23 minutes and 15 seconds on average to regain complete focus after a distraction. This finding, from a study by Gloria Mark, a professor at the University of California Irvine, highlights how interruptions, even short ones, can significantly delay productivity. Beyond lost time, consider the energy it takes to refocus and reenter a state of flow. Even if you're 33 percent better than the average, that's still 16 minutes per distraction—16 minutes of energy being diverted away from your goals. Not only does productivity suffer, but think of the energy it takes to regain that mental focus. Every ounce of energy spent regaining focus is energy you can no longer use to perform at your best when it truly matters. Over time, these repeated losses add up, leaving you less equipped to show up as your best self. One critical realization we've come to is that we often attempt to split our energy across too many tasks or distractions, spreading ourselves too thin and undermining our ability to excel.

Knowing how costly each distraction is, I challenge my clients and ask how many times they check their email per day. Usually the response is, "I check it throughout the entire day." I get the most resistance when I say, "We're going to change your email strategy, and it's going to bring you more energy." Initially, the excitement is off the charts—people respond with enthusiasm, asking, "Fantastic! What do we have to do?" Then I tell them: "You're going to check your email only twice a day." That's when I can practically hear the thump of someone falling out of their chair. If we're on the phone, the response is almost always the same: "I'm sorry, we're going to do what?"

The energy shifts in that moment—and not always in a positive way. When I say, "You'll only check your email twice a day," the reaction is often a mix of disbelief and hesitation. The first email check should be in the morning, focusing on the information you need to send out and anything critical you depend on. After that, we avoid email until later in the day—toward the end, when our energy is lower. At that point, you can block out a dedicated chunk of time to respond to and manage emails.

For some clients, I recommend an additional quick midday check, but only for essential information. Why is this so important? Why are we talking about email when discussing how we show up? Because how we show up is directly tied to the amount of energy we have—something we've already established. When we split our focus by constantly reacting to incoming emails, we're not just losing time. As we mentioned earlier, the cost of each distraction is 23 minutes and 15 seconds. Added up, that's a significant drain on your energy and productivity, which affects how effectively you can show up throughout the day.

What distracts you? Once you figure out your distractions, you have to deal with them. Here are some easy things to help you:

- Create a distraction-free environment.
- Set specific work and break times ((45 minutes of deep focus, a 10-minute recharge (change environment or change physical state), and five minutes to refocus)). For some, it is a 50-minute block and a five-to-five ratio. Do what is best for you.
- Limit digital distractions. These give your energy away (like flushing money down the toilet).
- Communicate boundaries to others.
- Set two to three 45-minute blocks (if possible) per day for flow-state deep-focus work.
- Prioritize and plan, as it limits drain during transitions and allows for better focus.
- Use music to focus you. Music significantly affects mood, and your mood affects your energy, which is depleted throughout the day.

Aligning Connection with the Energy Formula

A significant amount of energy is directly tied to your mindset. Earlier in the book, I introduced the energy formula: $E = MC^2$. At the time, I explained it as energy equals mindset multiplied by our choices[2]—with those choices rooted in confidence. But what if we reimagined the formula? What if we swapped the "C" for Connection? How might that change the way we approach energy?

Let's break it down: energy is driven by your mindset, multiplied by the choices you make, and amplified by the connections you cultivate. And here's the key—how you show up directly influences the quality of those connections. If you want to *crush it* in life, you need to ask yourself some tough but transformative questions:

- What kind of energy am I bringing to each connection?
- How am I showing up—not just physically, but emotionally and mentally?

- Am I fully present and engaged in the moment, or am I distracted, rushing through interactions with my mind elsewhere?

True energy doesn't just come from within; it's also generated by the way you interact with others and the world around you. Your connections—whether personal, professional, or even fleeting—are a mirror reflecting your energy back at you.

Sometimes, relationships or high levels of stress can drain our energy. That's why I always ask two key questions:

1. "What kind of energy do you bring?"
2. "What energy do you need to protect?"

Protecting your energy is essential because when it's compromised, everything else suffers. For some people, a hit to their emotional energy leaves them physically drained and unable to concentrate or focus. For others, when their mental energy drops, they can't focus, which in turn saps their emotional strength. It's crucial to identify which type of energy is most important to you and prioritize protecting it. Without that awareness, you can't "bring the juice" because if your energy is depleted or constantly drained, there's simply no juice left to bring.

The better your mindset, the stronger your choices, and the more intentional your connections, the more energy you'll have to fuel your journey.

So, let's tweak the formula and apply it: $\mathbf{E = M \times C^2}$, where connection and intentionality magnify everything else. If you want to create unstoppable energy, start by showing up—fully, authentically, and with purpose—for every connection in your life. Because when you bring your best self to the table, the energy you give multiplies, and the energy you receive in return becomes limitless.

Apply this to everything in your life—whether it's a one-on-one connection, a team meeting, your engagement with this book, your workouts, morning meditation, or even something as simple as washing the dishes. Every action, no matter how big or small, is an opportunity to show up with intention and energy. When you're fully present, you elevate the experience. Conversations become more meaningful. Team meetings become more productive. Workouts become transformative. Even mundane tasks like doing the dishes can feel purposeful when you approach them with the right mindset and focus.

The truth is, how you do anything is how you do everything. Your energy, mindset, and connection form the foundation for how you engage with the world, no matter the context. The challenge is to bring all of yourself to each moment—fully focused, fully intentional, and fully alive. That's how you build momentum and align your energy with your goals. How you show up profoundly impacts the quality of your connections, your authenticity, and the depth of your engagement. Research shows that one of the things we all seek is higher levels of engagement in our lives. By being mindful of how you show up, you can add greater depth, quality, and fulfillment to every experience and every interaction. Whether it's with others or within yourself, intentionality changes everything.

- **Mental Health:** Strong social connections significantly reduce the risk of depression and anxiety. People who feel connected to others tend to experience lower stress levels and have a more positive outlook on life (Holt-Lunstad, 2010).
- **Physical Health:** Research from Harvard's long-running study on adult development found that close relationships are associated with better physical health outcomes, including a lower risk of chronic diseases like heart disease. Social support has been shown to boost immune function and reduce inflammation (Vaillant & Waldinger, 2015).
- **Longevity:** Social connection has a significant impact on lifespan. Research suggests that a lack of social connection can be as detrimental to health as smoking 15 cigarettes a day (Holt-Lunstad et al., 2015).
- **Subjective Well-Being:** Research has consistently shown that relationships are one of the most important factors for happiness. The Harvard Study of Adult Development found that those most satisfied with their relationships in their 50s were the healthiest in their 80s (Waldinger, 2015).

- **Positive Psychology:** Engaging with others is one of the "PERMA" model components, a framework developed by psychologist Martin Seligman that highlights the five key elements of happiness: Positive Emotion, Engagement, Relationships, Meaning, and Accomplishment (Seligman, 2011).
- **Coping with Adversity:** Research published in *Health Psychology* found that people with strong social connections can better cope with stress and recover more quickly from trauma or significant life changes (Uchino, 2004).

This research underscores the importance of being present in our interactions. Ask yourself:

- Am I fully present at dinner, or is my phone in hand?
- Do I give my full attention when someone enters my office, or am I distracted?
- What energy am I bringing to each connection in my life?

How we show up defines the quality of our relationships, the depth of our interactions, and ultimately, the strength of our social connections.

PART III: "Be Here Now"

A powerful lesson I learned from spending time around future first-ballot Hall of Famer Drew Brees and other high performers is the transformative impact of being fully present. I call it **BE HERE NOW**. It's more than just showing up physically—it's about bringing your full attention, focus, and energy to the moment. When I'm fully present with someone, I'm not just offering my energy; I'm actively helping them feel energized through the connection we create. It's an exchange, a synergy that amplifies the interaction for both people. But this presence doesn't just benefit others—it's a two-way street. At the same time that we're giving energy, we're also recharging ourselves. Those moments of genuine connection become a source of renewal. The deeper and healthier the connection, the greater its ability to refill our energy reserves.

If we think of energy as capital or a resource, then relationships—especially meaningful, authentic ones—become one of the most valuable investments we can make. Like a bank account, these connections allow for deposits and withdrawals, enabling us to draw on them during times of need. A conversation where we truly feel heard, a heartfelt laugh, or even a silent moment of understanding can all be forms of replenishment. Being fully present isn't just a skill; it's a mindset, a choice to engage with life and people in a way that prioritizes quality over quantity. Whether it's a one-on-one conversation, a team huddle, or a quick moment with a loved one, the act of being present transforms those interactions into opportunities for growth, support, and energy renewal. In a world full of distractions, choosing to BE HERE NOW isn't just impactful—it's essential.

Being here now protects our energy by helping us eliminate distractions, becoming more aware of our transitions, and purposefully and consciously replenishing our energy as we go through the day. This also allows us to bring that incredible amount of energy to our connections as we engage with and interact with others. When we create that energy and bring the juice, an astonishing number of things happen. People feel valued, heard, and empowered because of your ability to focus solely on them. Sounds challenging? Take a step back and think about the last time someone gave you their undivided attention, when they truly locked in and listened to everything you shared. How did that make you feel? Bringing this energy also means being able to generate this on a consistent basis.

Let me state it again. Energy is our single most precious commodity. It is the foundation of productivity and performance and the currency of connection and relationships, as relationships thrive on emotional energy. When drained, it becomes harder to support, connect, or even listen actively to others. It is the resource we should work to protect so much better than we do. It is more important than money, our finances, our jobs. It is the single most vital thing to protect. Energy is the foundational commodity that powers all facets of life—from productivity and relationships to resilience and fulfillment. It allows us to maintain our health and drive our effectiveness. When managed wisely, it becomes a self-sustaining resource that enhances every dimension of our well-being and success. Prioritizing energy is not just a personal advantage; it is the core element that enables us to contribute meaningfully to ourselves and others.

Let me put it this way: you could have all the courage in the world, develop world-class resilience, and build an elite mindset with an unstoppable identity. But without the ability to generate the energy you need, you'll inevitably fall back into old patterns and behaviors. When your energy is depleted, resilience fades, and courage becomes harder to summon. Simply put, without energy, it's nearly impossible to sustain your progress and maintain your strength.

Transforming The Energy

I've always loved being in NFL meeting rooms, watching which coaches could instantly command respect the moment they walked in. Sean Payton was one of the best. He had a presence that demanded attention—not through intimidation, but through the way he carried himself and the energy he brought into the room. When you gather a group of 22- to 28-year-olds for an NFL training camp, it's inevitable that the time between on-field sessions—especially during team meetings—is filled with chatter, jokes, and playful banter. Having been blessed to sit in so many NFL rooms and meeting spaces, I've found it fascinating to observe which coaches can truly transform that energy. Some have an incredible ability to channel all that noise into focus, purpose, and momentum, creating a unique atmosphere that sets the tone for greatness.

When a coach walks up to the front of the room, takes the podium, and says, "Alright, everyone, let's get started. Lock it in, focus, and quiet down," it's one thing. But when someone like Sean Payton walks into the room, it's a completely different experience. He doesn't have to say a word—his presence alone transforms the energy. The room naturally quiets, focus sharpens, and attention shifts to him. That's the power of great leadership. The best leaders don't just respond to the energy in the room—they transform it. There is a quote that reminds me of this: "True leaders don't have to demand leadership." Think about Oprah Winfrey, Nelson Mandela, or Tony Robbins. These are people who have mastered the ability to shift the energy of a space and elevate those around them. They set the tone, create momentum, and inspire action, often without needing to demand it. It's a skill that goes beyond authority. It's about presence, intention, and the ability to connect deeply with those in the room.

This concept of transforming energy is something we coach extensively. It's not just about commanding attention; it's about creating an environment where people feel engaged, inspired, and ready to rise to the occasion. So ask yourself:

- How are you transforming the energy in the spaces you enter?
- How do you show up when you walk into a room?
- How are you creating and shaping the energy you want?

Whether it's a team meeting, a family dinner, or a one-on-one conversation, the energy you bring has the power to influence everyone around you. The best leaders know this, and they use it to create lasting impact.

Dr. Kevin Elko, in his book *Believing is Seeing*, wrote about how thermometers respond to the circumstances around them. They go up or down depending on the environment. A lot of us operate like thermometers. However, the great ones, the best leaders, function as a thermostat. They set the temperature and the climate for the room. They know how to adjust the thermostat settings. Create that environment we want with our energy, whether with our loved ones, a team we lead, or even with the lady or the gentleman checking us out at the cash line.

Everything in life comes down to transforming energy, whether it's coaching at Georgetown Prep or leading a team to a CFL championship. The principle is the same: how you show up matters, and the energy you bring has the power to shape outcomes in ways you might not immediately see. I started my coaching journey at Georgetown Prep, and I'll never forget the lesson I learned at the end of my first season. It was my first real experience as a football coach, and like any coach, I poured everything I had into my players—showing up fully for them, pushing them, and believing in their potential.

At the end of the season, one young man came up to me and said,

"Coach, I want to thank you for everything, you really helped me through a difficult time."

I was caught off guard. I looked at him and said, "Oh man, I'm so proud of you. You worked so hard, and you gave me everything you had."

He said, "No, no, no, Coach, that's not what I'm talking about. I want to thank you because you helped me solve a huge problem in my life."

I take a step back, and my wheels are turning. And I am like, this young man never came up and talked to me. He never shared anything with me. *Had I forgotten something? Did I miss something?* He must have seen the perplexed look in my eyes because he said, "No, Coach, I never came and told you what was going on, but you helped me fix it just by how you showed up every day for us."

His words were a reminder of the unseen impact we can have when we truly show up for others. As a young coach, that was one of the most potent lessons I could have ever been given or blessed with. How many people are watching you and learning from you? This young man said, "No matter what happened, Coach, win or lose, you showed up with the same energy and consistency every day. You were as excited when we won and as positive as possible after we had struggled."

It wouldn't be till years later that I found out that this wonderful young man had been contemplating suicide. Whether it's high school football or the CFL championship, the principle remains the same: the energy you bring as a leader, a coach, or even just as a person showing up in someone's life is transformative. Sometimes, that impact is hidden from us—we don't always see it immediately. But when you're fully present and intentional about the energy you create and share, you set the stage for others to rise to their best. It's not just about wins or losses, titles, or accolades. It's about those moments when someone looks at you and says, "Thank you." That's when you know you've transformed more than just a game—you've transformed lives. That is what coaching is all about.

Fast forward to the 2016 Grey Cup. After warm-ups wrapped up, we all headed back to the locker room, and I pulled out my second call sheet. For those unfamiliar, the call sheet is essentially the coach's tailored "playbook" for that specific game. It contains all the plays and

THE CRUSH-IT FORMULA

strategies for different scenarios—red zone situations, goal-line defense, when you're backed up near your own goal line, and every other critical moment in between. It's where the magic happens, the "secret sauce" of the game plan. This second call sheet was prepared specifically for the backup quarterback, just in case we needed to make a change. And as we reviewed it, we adjusted our mindset. We told ourselves, *It's all right. The game still has to be played.* I reassured the team, "Here's the plan—we're in good shape." Everyone nodded in agreement, but you could still feel it—that underlying tension hanging in the air. The energy in the room had shifted, and not in a good way.

With a coin toss underway, I looked at Trevor, our backup quarterback, and saw quiet confidence in his eyes. He was ready to go. He was locked in and had a belief in himself. However, all of a sudden, running out of the locker room came Henry "Hank" Burris. The energy in that stadium and on our sideline was transformed. Great leaders can do that, and Henry, like Drew Brees, was a great leader.

It works the other way, too, unfortunately. In 2018, we were back in the CFL championship game, the opponent was the same, the Calgary Stampeders, and the only thing different was the location. Our game was being played in Edmonton, Alberta, the northernmost city in North America with a population of over one million.

The day before the game, we held a "walk-through" on the field, a standard practice to assess conditions like footing, sun angles, and wind. When we stepped onto the field, we were greeted with a sheet of ice. Players were slipping and sliding all over the place, and it immediately created a sense of dread in me. I made sure no one saw or felt my unease, but deep down, I was worried. We were a "big" team with tall receivers, players who would struggle to change directions on such a slick surface compared to those with a lower center of gravity. League officials assured us that the ice would melt before game time. They were wrong.

In one of the worst displays of field conditions I've ever witnessed, both teams struggled from the start. However, just before halftime, we hit a massive 70-plus-yard pass with 30 seconds left, giving us a much-needed spark. Moments like that—a big play in football or a victory in business—do wonders for momentum, and we had it back. We scored with 2:15 left in the half, quickly stopped Calgary, and even had another chance to score before the break. But two missed opportunities forced us to punt the ball back with just 7 seconds remaining. That's when Calgary struck with a crushing 97-yard punt return for a touchdown. Just like that, we went from trailing 14-11 to being down 21-11 heading into halftime. The energy had shifted dramatically, and not in our favor.

Where we failed as a team was at halftime. A lack of clarity about the conditions and uncertainty about what plays we could execute effectively seeped into the locker room, transforming the energy in a negative way. We came out for the second half hesitant and unsure. Despite fighting hard the rest of the game, the momentum had already slipped away. The opportunity to transform the energy was either missed or not taken advantage of. We ultimately lost 27-16.

The lesson? Energy, confidence, and clarity are everything in moments of adversity. If you can't stabilize and transform the energy when it matters most, the game—or any opportunity—can quickly slip out of your hands.

Showing Up with Authenticity and Curiosity

Showing up with authenticity is about more than simply being present, making eye contact, and giving someone your attention. To truly make an impact, you need genuine curiosity and a sincere investment in the person in front of you and their experiences in that moment. Authenticity isn't about performing or proving—it's about showing up as your true self and creating meaningful connections.

Think of it like building a house. The foundation represents your core—your values, beliefs, and sense of identity. It's the unseen but essential structure that keeps everything steady and strong. When you show up authentically, you rely on this solid foundation, allowing you to engage with others without feeling the need to insert your point of view or say something to validate yourself. From there, the walls, windows, and roof represent how you connect with the world around you. A well-built house invites others in, offering a space of warmth, safety, and belonging. When we show up authentically, we create a similar space for those around us. People feel comfortable, understood, and valued when they step into that "house" we've built with trust and integrity.

This kind of presence naturally draws people in and creates a desire to be near you, learn from you, and build with you. That ability to create genuine connections and inspire trust is what separates great leaders, mentors, and friends from the rest. And the truth is, we all have the ability to do this. When we create a space where others feel welcomed and valued, we nurture the relationships in our lives. This deepens our connections and allows us to bring the right kind of energy into every interaction. Sometimes, this means showing up with passionate energy and excitement, like the energy I carried onto the football field for years. Other times, it means showing up with quiet strength, calm support, or thoughtful listening. Authenticity and genuine curiosity are like the foundation and walls of that house. Together, they create a structure where trust and connection thrive. And when you show up in this way, you bring the kind of energy that transforms not just relationships, but lives.

How can we improve this skill? I will share several small but important pieces to connecting that are often overlooked:

- **Share laughter.** Laughter is a universal language that bridges gaps and brings people closer together. Research shows that sharing humor effectively fosters a sense of connection and strengthens relationships. Laughter creates a positive emotional experience that binds people, even across differences. Look for moments of lightness and shared joy—it's a powerful way to connect. We all need to laugh more. Think about how this makes you feel when you laugh with someone. It's powerful!
- **Don't judge.** Andy Reid, one of the winningest football coaches of all time, summarized his coaching philosophy in two words. Don't judge. This is so powerful. And simple.
- **Share positive emotions.** A phenomenon called positivity resonance occurs when two people feel and express joyous emotions together. This creates an upward spiral of feeling that can occur when we are together more so than when we are alone.
- **Be vulnerable.** We discussed this in the courage section, and it shows up here again. Want to really connect with others on a different level? Be vulnerable. Many people

underestimate the role vulnerability plays in connecting with others. Sharing your authentic self—your thoughts, feelings, and even insecurities—opens the door for genuine connection. It encourages others to do the same and creates a sense of mutual trust and understanding.

- **Approach each opportunity to connect with the sole purpose of connecting.** One of the most overlooked aspects of connection is the intention behind it. Too often, people enter conversations with an agenda, focusing on what they'll say next, how they'll come across, or how to make themselves relevant. To truly connect, you need to set aside your agenda and engage with the sole purpose of being present for the other person. Approach every opportunity to connect with the mindset of BEING HERE NOW. Focus entirely on the other person, what they're saying, how they're feeling, and what they need at that moment. Showing up fully for others, without distraction, transforms the interaction from transactional to transformational. We are all busy, with countless things vying for our attention, but when we treat conversations as tasks to check off a list, we miss the opportunity to create meaningful moments. By shifting your mindset to prioritize connection over transaction, you not only deepen relationships but also generate energy that uplifts both you and the people around you.

Connection isn't just about what you say or do; it's about how you show up—genuinely, fully, and with an open heart. By incorporating these small yet powerful practices into your daily life, you can strengthen your relationships, transform your energy, and create meaningful, lasting bonds with others. And remember, there is no one right way to connect.

Different situations call for different types of energy, and the ability to adapt to those moments is a critical part of showing up authentically and a huge part of leadership. Some conversations require compassionate energy—a quiet, empathetic presence that allows others to feel safe and supported. Other times, a situation demands confident energy, where a strong, decisive presence inspires trust and provides clarity in moments of uncertainty. In my former days as a football coach, I've learned the importance of adapting my energy to the situation. Sometimes, it was about bringing passionate energy to fire up a team, rallying them to push through challenges. Other times, it was about projecting calm, collected energy to steady the team and help them focus under pressure. Recognizing what the moment demands and being able to adjust accordingly can be the difference between success and failure.

When we become more in tune with the energy a situation requires, we gain the ability to shift and shape it intentionally. This isn't just about reacting to what's happening around us; it's about actively understanding the energy dynamics at play and consciously choosing the approach that will create the most positive and productive outcome. Mastering this skill allows us to bring the right energy into play at the right time, elevating not just ourselves but everyone around us.

This skill requires you to not only sense those energy shifts but to address them and transform them in real time. Imagine walking into a room where tension hangs thick in the air. Instead of being swept up in that energy, you have the opportunity to bring calm and reassurance, resetting the tone for everyone involved. On the other hand, if you step into a moment that lacks enthusiasm or drive, you can inject energy, excitement, and focus to reignite momentum.

One of my coaches, Andrea, once shared a perfect example of this. She described walking into a room where people were laughing, one of those deep, uncontrollable belly laughs. You know, the kind where they can't even stop long enough to tell you what's so funny? What usually happens next? You ask, "What's so funny?" And even before they answer, their laughter becomes contagious, and you start laughing, too. In that moment, the energy shifts, and suddenly, everyone feels lighter and more connected. I experienced something similar one night while putting my daughter to bed. She got a case of the "giggles"—a code-red situation for any parent trying to enforce bedtime. But this time, I couldn't help it—I got the giggles, too. We literally couldn't stop laughing. It went on and on for about 10 or 11 minutes, and by the end, we were completely exhausted. Even as I write this, I can't help but laugh all over again!

This kind of awareness takes practice. It means choosing to be present enough to feel the shifts in energy around you and intentional enough to choose how you respond. Mastering this ability allows you to meet people where they are, elevate the energy when needed, and create meaningful connections that leave a lasting impact. Ultimately, showing up isn't just about being present—it's about *how* you're present. The energy you bring into a room has the power to shift outcomes, foster connection, and inspire action. By cultivating this awareness and learning to adjust and transform energy in the moment, you'll not only deepen your relationships but also elevate the impact you have on every situation you encounter.

Living Life as a Sprinter, Not a Marathoner

For years, we've been told that life is a marathon, but I challenge that expression. While I deeply respect marathon runners and their incredible ability to endure 26.2 miles (or compete in multiple marathons), I believe this analogy misses something crucial about how life really works. Picture a marathon runner: they're usually thin and long, their faces often showing the strain of sustaining such a grueling effort. Their bodies are conditioned for endurance, sacrificing explosiveness for stamina.

Now, contrast that image with a sprinter—think of icons like Usain Bolt, Marion Jones, or Ben Johnson. When you picture them, you likely see powerful legs, vibrant smiles, and energy radiating off of them. Sprinters don't look depleted; they look alive, dynamic, and powerful. Life, I believe, is not one long, continuous race. Instead, life is a series of sprints—short bursts of focused energy followed by intentional recovery. What do the best sprinters do? They sprint, and then they recharge. They sprint again, recharge, and repeat the process. Their performance doesn't rely solely on how fast they can run—it also depends on how effectively they can recover and prepare for the next sprint. This is where the lesson applies to our own lives. This is how we should be living not only every day but within our days.

If you want to CRUSH-IT, it means knowing how to show up fully in each moment—with genuine curiosity, focused energy, and meaningful connection. Showing up isn't just about being present; it's about bringing your best self to the table every time. But to sustain this level of performance, you must also know how to replenish your energy after each "sprint." You can't give your best if you're running on empty, and you can't thrive if your "juice" is depleted. Success is about mastering the balance between showing up powerfully and recharging purposefully so you can keep bringing that energy to every challenge and opportunity. This means you must have good habits. After all, you cannot generate the energy needed on a potato chip-only diet.

CHAPTER 5
HIGH PERFORMING HABITS

The first four chapters of this book were all about the internal aspect of CRUSH-IT. **Courage, Resilience, Unstoppability**, and how you **Show Up**. These qualities are internal. The next one, the "H" in CRUSH-IT, is externally focused—**High Performing Habits**.

We are going to take a look at some habits, particularly high-performing habits. Habits like eating right, getting enough sleep, and exercising are all important habits, but what I am going to focus on are the habits that are needed to elevate your game. They are the difference makers that help individuals achieve mastery and sustained elite performance. We will explore each of these aspects in depth throughout this chapter.

- Mastery Over Success
- Relentless Consistency
- Investing in Your Best Asset
- The Art of Selective Attention
- Harnessing the Power of Visualization
- Surround Yourself with Game-Changers
- Clarity Simplifies Everything
- Integrity: The Core of True Excellence

MASTERY OVER SUCCESS

There's a powerful scene in the movie *The Last Samurai* where Nathan Algren, played by Tom Cruise, reflects on his time living in Katsumoto's village in Japan. Having spent a few weeks immersed in their culture, he is struck by something extraordinary: the unwavering dedication to mastery that every single individual in the village displays. Whether it's a swordsmith forging a blade, a farmer tending to crops, or a warrior practicing kata with precision, each person is fully committed to their craft.

Algren is captivated by their focus, discipline, and intentionality. Every action, no matter how small, is carried out with purpose and attention to detail. It's as though the people of the village view their work not just as tasks to complete but as an expression of their character and a way to honor their role in the community. Their dedication is deeply tied to their values and their sense of identity, creating a culture where mastery isn't just about skill, but about living with integrity and respect for the process. This level of commitment and presence is rare in the modern world, where distractions are constant, and people often multitask their way through life. Algren's amazement serves as a reminder of what it means to truly show up for something, to bring focus, passion, and intentionality to every moment, no matter how routine it may seem. It's not just about perfecting the skill; it's about honoring the journey toward mastery and bringing your full self to whatever you do.

Early in my football career, I had the privilege of working for Marc Trestman, former head coach of the Chicago Bears as well as Coach of the Year in the CFL and a disciple of Bill Walsh, one of the most legendary and successful coaches in the history of football. He shared wisdom that has stuck with me ever since. He said, "Jaime, you have to focus on the process, not the outcome. You will never be able to fully control the outcome, but you can control the process and focus on a standard of performance." These concepts—process over outcome and maintaining a standard of performance—were ingrained in me early on in my football journey.

Looking back, I can see that when I fully embraced this mindset, I thrived. At times, it felt like I was crushing it, fully aligned with these principles. But there were also moments when I unintentionally strayed from them, and it felt as though I'd never been taught them at all. The difference was undeniable. Marc played a key role in my development as a football coach and remains a close friend today.

What I've come to realize is that success lies in the process of mastery. It's about living in the details—focusing on mastering your craft, refining your skills, shaping your thoughts, exercising patience, and cultivating your self-talk. And this is a commitment you must make. It's not a one-time or occasional thing. A personal commitment to choose mastery. When you shift your attention away from obsessing over the outcome and instead commit to the process of improving and growing every day, that's where real success and clarity begin to unfold. It's in the process, not the result, that you find the insight and fulfillment you're looking for.

RELENTLESS CONSISTENCY

While in season for 22 years, my alarm would go off at 4:30 a.m., and for those same 22 years, every day, I would wake up at 4:30 and get myself into the office by 5 a.m.—no snooze button. I needed some extra sleep mentality, but consistent dedication in this area of my life was more important. It did not feel like it then, but looking back on it, I am proud of that. It was not easy. However, after repeated, consistent action, it became natural, so much so that the alarm never woke my wife; my body naturally woke up around 4:27 a.m., before the alarm would even go off.

Earlier in this book, we talked about "call sheets" in football. There's an entire process and art to putting these together. As the week progresses, the game plan gets finalized, and then the real work of assembling the call sheet begins. When everyone left the facility the day before the game, I, as the offensive coordinator, would close the door to my office and spend the next six hours finalizing the call sheet.

> To access an example
> of a Call Sheet
>
> **SCAN THE QR CODE:**

When you look at the call sheet, you'll notice different colors, highlighted areas, sharpie marks scattered throughout, items circled, and reminders written in all kinds of ways. My wife used to joke that I played with crayons all day, and looking back at these sheets, she might have been right!

I loved this time. When the building was quiet, and I had the space to arrange the call sheet exactly how I wanted, I could fully envision the game ahead. I went through every "forgotten" or overlooked area of the game plan that other coaches didn't have to worry about, or those "gotta have it" moments—scenarios like when the game is on the line, and you need to score from the two-yard line, the 10-yard line, or when there's just one play left from the 25-yard line. All of these special situations, and so many more, had to go on that sheet. No matter how drained I was or how much I wanted to head home to see my family (who I often hadn't seen all week due to the demanding 5 a.m. to 11 p.m. schedule), I was relentless about this process. As you know, at times, I even prepared two separate call sheets for different quarterbacks. I prided myself on that consistency.

Every week, no matter if we were at home or on the road, if it was a short week or a long one between games, I followed this process. This relentless commitment to detail and preparation was one of the reasons we led the league year after year in several key statistical categories. The consistency in my approach wasn't just about getting the call sheet "right"—it was about creating a foundation for success, week in and week out. What I realized through this process is how consistency, over time, becomes more than just an action—it becomes a habit. When you commit to showing up consistently in a specific area, it stops being something you have to think about and starts becoming part of who you are. It creates a rhythm and a sense of reliability that others can count on, whether it's your team, your family, or even yourself.

I'm currently working with a company to help them create a growth-oriented culture, and one of the first initiatives I started with the leadership team was crafting a daily text message. Each morning, they receive a message designed to inspire and focus them for the day ahead. One of the C-suite executives commented on the remarkable consistency of these messages—the fact that they arrived every single day, without fail (well, except Sundays—they get those off). This daily practice not only reinforced the importance of consistency in their own roles but also highlighted the need for consistent messaging with their employees.

Now, I'll be the first to admit that I'm not as consistent in all areas of my life as I'd like to be. But one of my goals is to be exceptionally and relentlessly consistent in the areas that matter most—driving growth, inspiring change, and creating a meaningful impact on others. I'm always looking for ways to refine and improve my own consistency. Like everyone else, I'm a work in progress, but I believe that consistency is one of the most powerful tools for lasting growth and transformation. The key is this: consistency doesn't just reinforce habits—it builds momentum. The more consistent you are, the more you reinforce not just actions but a mindset of progress and reliability. It's not just what you do—it's who you become. And that's the real power of turning consistency into a habit.

INVESTING IN YOUR BEST ASSET

Game day in pro football is, in many ways, the easiest day of the week. The adrenaline is up, the joy of the victory from last week or the pain from the loss has eroded; you have another opportunity. Game day is the culmination of your work, the ridiculous hours, the arguments and disagreements that come from game planning, and being around over 100 alpha males every week, each with their vision of how things should be. Now, what's cool to experience is how the excitement of the game starts to turn into something different. Excited energy becomes nervous energy. *Have I covered everything? Are the players locked in today? How will we respond? What will I do if our quarterback struggles? What if a key starter has tested positive for COVID-19?*

I remember one game day, I was sitting in the drive-through of Starbucks, waiting for my tall blonde—easy, wife, as you read this, a cup of blonde coffee. On this particular game day, I didn't feel the usual excitement. I was miserable. I was the head coach and offensive coordinator of the Edmonton Elks in the CFL. The season started poorly, and I realized I needed a coach. The thought came and stuck with me. I had been coaching for years but never invested in someone to help *me*. I knew I lacked aspects of my growth, things that would make me a more effective leader, more effective, help me gain more clarity, address my blind spots, and help me chart a course for improvement. I knew it in my soul: I needed someone and thought I would research someone that weekend. Then I drove off, and my mind moved on to prepping the last few precious details for the game. We lost that game, and we lost it badly. I was embarrassed. As the head coach, it was my responsibility to show everyone how to handle the fallout—with grace, accountability, and strength. I told myself I'd take the blame. But instead of addressing the deeper issue, I pushed it aside. The thought of hiring additional help crossed my mind, but I dismissed it with, *"I don't have the time for that. I have bigger problems to solve. I need to fix this myself."* We won the next two games, which only masked the underlying problem even further. It was a temporary bandage over a much larger wound. Looking back, in 2021, I failed as the head coach of that team.

Failure, especially when it's tied to a lifelong dream, hits hard. It forces a process of deep self-reflection. I found myself drowning in doubt, questioning everything. *Why did this happen to me? How could I have let this happen?* The weight of those questions was crushing, but they also forced me to confront truths I had been avoiding. Failure isn't just about the mistakes—it's about what you choose to do next.

Those harsh feelings lingered for weeks. But soon, I started applying principles and turning them into action. I began an Excel sheet of the lessons learned, and one of those lessons that stood out was the importance of getting a coach and having one in your life. For 22 years, I have been coaching individuals to achieve high performance, succeed, rise to new levels, rise above their mental doubts, and elevate their game. However, I had never prioritized elevating my own performance by surrounding myself with a team of people who could identify my blind spots—limiting beliefs, misaligned behaviors, or areas where I needed growth. In high performance, so much of the focus is on taking intentional action, shaping thoughts, and building or breaking patterns—patterns that either propel us toward greatness or hold us back. Yet, I began to realize that the very thing I valued most—developing an incredible mindset and helping others craft theirs—was something I had neglected in my own life. I had overlooked not just my mindset but a host of other areas I needed to improve. It was a wake-up call, a moment of clarity that reminded me even the best need help to stay on top of their game.

This has been my passion and love since I was a kid. I was always fascinated by what the best athletes, businesses, companies, and individuals did to achieve those incredible levels of success. In short, I was a high-performance nerd. I always gravitated to how you unlock your best self and truly develop elite levels of performance, an environment of growth, and a mindset of achievement. Despite all my extensive study in high performance, even earning my undergraduate degree in neuroscience (do not ask me how this led to law school) to understand the connection between brain processes and real-world outcomes, I kept coming back to a fundamental question: can you truly build high-performance habits? Are they a skill you can develop or merely an innate strength some people naturally have? So, for the first time, I decided to hire a high-performance coach, and it was one of the best decisions I have ever made.

The transformations I began to see almost immediately were both impactful and unsettling. They weren't entirely encouraging because they came with the realization that I might have waited too long to hire a coach—too long to pursue the next levels of growth in my career. For years, I had been trying to do it all myself—or at least convincing myself that I was.

As I reflected on this, I leaned into one of my strengths: my ability to adapt and pivot. I embraced a sense of calm and adjustment and began applying that mindset to building habits. Over the next few years, through coaching, I discovered just how powerful key habits can be. These habits have the potential to elevate not just your performance but your entire approach to growth and success. They became the foundation for unlocking a higher level of achievement I hadn't thought possible.

One of those habits that highest performers have is having a very intentional plan for their growth, and they have learned that the greatest investment you can ever make is in yourself and your development. Being intentional about your growth means being proactive. In football, when a player gets hurt, he goes into rehab, similar to when someone is trying to recover. Receiving coaching for me initially was like rehab, I wasn't hurt, so I didn't need it. The best teams have sports science programs that include what is known as "pre-hab." The idea is simple: instead of repairing damage after it's done, focus on strengthening and preparing areas of the body to prevent injuries in the first place, especially areas that are weak. That concept is how I see certain aspects of coaching. It's not about fixing what's broken—it's about building the skills you'll need tomorrow so you have them when the moment arrives, rather than scrambling to create them on the spot.

Coaching helps you see your blind spots before they become problems. It helps you develop the right kind of self-talk, build unshakable confidence, reframe limiting beliefs, and create an intentional plan for growth *before* you're forced into "rehab" for those areas. It's about preparation—pre-hab for your personal and professional development.

So, let me ask: Do you have a deliberate plan for your growth? I'm not talking about simply setting goals—I mean a well-thought-out strategy for your development that includes:

- **Skill building**: Identifying and strengthening the core skills you need.
- **Self-reflection**: Regularly assessing your progress and adjusting as needed.
- **Mindset development**: Cultivating resilience, confidence, and intentional self-talk.
- **Energy and time management**: Learning to optimize your focus and balance.
- **Behavioral habit formation**: Establishing consistent, productive habits.
- **Purpose and values alignment**: Ensuring your actions are deeply rooted in what matters most to you.

How are you tapping into the deeper parts of yourself to uncover the drive and clarity to build this kind of plan? Pre-hab requires intention, commitment, and self-awareness, but it's the foundation for lasting growth and resilience. (More on this in Chapter 6.)

THE ART OF SELECTIVE ATTENTION

"Lock it in... Dammit! How many times am I going to have to repeat it?"

"I cannot seem to focus today."

"Why do I need to repeat myself? Weren't you listening?"

"Why can't I seem to remember things?"

"Sweetheart... I've told you three times to brush your teeth and get ready for bed!"

"Sorry, Daddy, I wasn't listening."

(The last one is a typical weekly conversation with my daughter.)

These words are familiar. You hear them on football fields, in boardrooms, and even in our homes. Focus and attention—two seemingly simple skills—are some of the hardest to master.

One of the most challenging aspects of being a play-caller in football (and I loved my 12-plus years of calling plays) is the sheer volume of stimuli you have to process in real time. Let me walk you through it. The play ends. Immediately, someone in the press box relays the situation through your headset: "Second down and seven from the left hash, 18-yard line." Now, you've got to find the plays you've prepared for that specific scenario while simultaneously ensuring the right personnel are on the field. You relay the play call to the quarterback, anticipate the potential outcomes of the next play, and start thinking ahead. All this while glancing at the defense to process their formation and tendencies —and keeping an eye on the play clock. It's a whirlwind of decisions and adjustments compressed into 35 seconds.

Here's a real-life example:

Coach in box: "Okay, hold on—third and two on the 18, right hash."

Me: "Are you sure it's two yards, not three?"

Coach in box: "Yes, it's two. Definitely two yards."

Me: "Okay. Give me 'Detroit' personnel."
Coaches around me: "Detroit, Detroit!" (This means double tight ends, or two tight ends.)
Me (to QB): "Let's go. Here's the play."
Head coach: "Jaime, keep it on the ground here. I don't want to give them time, but we need the first down."
Me: "Got it. Let's go Zac to 0 Up." (Part of the QB call.)
Running back coach: "Hey, Coach, Cory is down." (Cory is the key running back for the play.)
Me: *Signaling thumbs up.* "Do we have 11 in the huddle?"
Coach in box: "Yes."
Me: "Alright, here's the call: Z-Shift to 0 Up Fap Ride 34 Flash X-Smoke."
Trainer: "Jacobi's back up; he's okay." (Jacobi had been injured two plays earlier.)
Coach in box: "Wait, *shit*—they marked it as third and three, not two. It's three yards."
Me: "Hold on." (To QB) "I'm changing it."
Me (to head coach): "It's third and three. Do you still want to run it?"
Head coach: "Do what you have to do."
Me (to QB): "Okay, here's the call: 0 Up 66 Ice Gotti."
Coach in box: "Clock's at 10 seconds."
Head coach: "We're out of timeouts."
Me (to QB): "Clock's at five. Get it snapped!"

All of that happens in about 35 seconds. Not every play unfolds this way, but a high percentage of them do. Processing and managing all those stimuli is why I love football and why I respect the players and coaches who handle it daily.

Now, imagine being the quarterback in this scenario. Not only does he have to process the play call and relay it to the huddle, but he also has to break the huddle, identify the defense (finding the "Mike" linebacker), and answer rapid-fire questions from teammates: "What's the call again?" "Do I have a route or a block?" "Did you say 66 or 67?" And on top of all that, he has to snap the ball on time, read the defense as it shifts, and execute the play—all while 11 opponents are trying to bury him in the turf. This doesn't even account for carrying the emotional weight of the last play, or the fact that his head bounced on the turf two plays prior.

Selective attention and the ability to focus on the task at hand are skills that can be developed. The world's best performers don't leave this to chance; they turn focus into an intentional habit. Let me use a different example. As you may recall, I played tennis for years—at the college level and even in some lower-level professional events. Unlike football, tennis is entirely on you. No one is there to say, "We've got you," or to offer reassurance. It's just you out there. What I love about tennis, and what connects it to this discussion, is the way the best players manage their attention. Between points, they don't just reset physically—they reset mentally. They've developed repeated patterns, rituals, and processes that allow them to refocus and lock in. It's not just a skill; it's a habit.

This ability to focus and intentionally redirect your energy, whether on a football field, a tennis court, or in everyday life, is what separates good from great. And the good news? It's a skill anyone can develop with the right mindset and practice. Let's talk about how to develop it.

SHARPEN YOUR MIND: BRAIN TRAINING, BEATS, MINDFULNESS, AND INBOX FREEDOM

"Coach, you're going to love this. Here's how it works: I'm going to time you. Here's a sheet with arrows, and I want you to tell me the direction of these arrows as quickly as you can. Then, we're going to switch it up. You'll alternate—giving me the direction of the first arrow and the color of each alternating one. Ready, Coach?"

Trevor Harris, one of the quarterbacks I was fortunate to work with, introduced me to the concept of combat brain training through his work with John Kennedy. John has trained top athletes, U.S. Marines, and executives worldwide, helping them develop the ability to handle multiple stimuli without becoming overwhelmed. The idea is simple but powerful: at some point, we all "lock up" when faced with too much information. For some, it happens with just three stimuli. For example, imagine a dad driving with the music blasting, while his wife is telling him to take the next exit. At the same time, he realizes he's two lanes over. Three stimuli—the music, the need to take the exit, and the need to change lanes to do so—can cause a mental freeze. Everyone has a different threshold, but at some point, we all hit that limit. To help our players handle these situations better, we brought John in to work with them. His training was nothing short of incredible.

I went through combat brain training myself, and after experiencing firsthand how challenging it can be to process multiple stimuli, I quickly realized how much I needed it! The training taught me that while our brain has a natural limit on how much information it can process at once, we can increase this capacity with intentional development. Combat brain training doesn't teach multitasking; in fact, it's quite the opposite. It helps you filter and prioritize information more effectively.

Through this training, your brain starts acting like a mental filter, automatically focusing on the most important information while tuning out distractions and background noise. By pushing the limits of your cognitive load, you can enter a better state of flow and reduce unnecessary energy loss. Selective attention plays a big role here—it acts as a filter, preventing cognitive overload by prioritizing what's most relevant. Combat brain training enhances this ability, allowing you to stretch your limits intentionally, process more stimuli, and focus more efficiently. This isn't just about handling more—it's about handling it better. It's about developing a sharper mind that processes information purposefully, manages attention effectively, and thrives under pressure. It's a game-changer for anyone looking to level up their mental performance. For those interested, send me a message and I will connect you with John.

To connect with Jaime

SCAN THE QR CODE:

So, one key habit in high performance is the ability to sustain attention for extended periods of time rather than splitting your attention (called divided attention) or alternating your attention between different tasks. How are you building this skill out and turning it into a habit?

The world's best performers understand that focus isn't something that happens by accident—it's something they prioritize intentionally. They build focus time into their schedules, treating it as non-negotiable. It's not a vague concept; it's visible in their calendars, blocked off and protected, just like a meeting with a top client or a championship game. But it's not just about carving out the time—it's about knowing how to use it. High performers develop a process to center themselves and get into their zone or flow state, or the mental state where they perform at their absolute best. They understand that flow isn't triggered by chance; it's cultivated through deliberate action.

For some, this might involve a pre-focus ritual: a specific routine to signal to their brain that it's time to lock in. It could be as simple as meditation, deep breathing, or listening to a favorite playlist to set the tone. For others, it might include clearing their environment of distractions, organizing their workspace, or reviewing a clear set of goals for the session ahead.

The key is consistency. These routines become habits, and over time, they train the brain to slip into focus more quickly and deeply. By developing and sticking to these processes, high performers ensure they can maximize their productivity, creativity, and clarity during their focus time. Moreover, they treat this time as sacred. They don't allow interruptions, distractions, or non-essential tasks to creep in. They guard their focus time because they know it's the foundation for their success. Whether they're athletes, artists, or executives, this intentional approach to focus is what separates the good from the great. Do you have dedicated focus time in your schedule? Do you have a process to center yourself and get into your flow state? If not, what can you start doing today to make it a priority? Because focus isn't just a skill—it's the gateway to achieving your highest potential.

In football, we call it a pre-game ritual. The best football players use this process on game day and utilize it daily in practice. I could tell right away how detailed and focused a player was by watching his pre-game ritual. The elite, the best, have very structured routines to get into focus. They have a detailed plan from the moment they step on the field, sometimes up to two hours before kickoff. It's not just the routine that matters—it's the process they use to focus their mind to BE HERE NOW. Research shows that some background music can be a good antidote to other distractions, and additional research shows that your choice of music is influenced by your desire to enhance certain moods even when you are not conscious of it. So, what is it for you? What is your process for your pre-game? What steps do you take to prepare yourself to get into a focused state?

- Do you use a pre-game music mix to get into the right frame of mind?
- Do you meditate and focus on your breathing before diving into deep work?
- Do you close the door, sit in a dark room, and shut off all technology to eliminate distractions?
- Do you schedule focus time during your peak performance hours when you're most productive?
- In *Atomic Habits*, James Clear discusses using **anchor tasks**—assigning one main priority to each workday. This approach ensures you have one non-negotiable task to complete daily.
- Have you eliminated unnecessary email checking? Review your inbox once for urgent items and set aside a specific time later in the day to respond when deep focus isn't required.
- Do you manage your energy by taking regular breaks to recharge?
- Do you put your phone in another room or turn it off to minimize distractions and maintain focus?

The last piece to consider is environmental control. The world's best performers understand the significance of shaping their surroundings to maximize focus and productivity. It's incredibly challenging to maintain concentration when your environment works against you. Take a moment to reflect. What does your ideal environment need to look like? How should it feel—cozy, minimalistic, or highly organized? And what sounds or levels of silence help you concentrate best?

HARNESSING THE POWER OF VISUALIZATION

We touched on visualization earlier, and I want to revisit its importance and encourage making it a daily habit. If you already practice visualization regularly, feel free to move ahead. If not, stay with me—this is worth your time.

The ability to sit in stillness is closely tied to the skill of visualizing ourselves in different scenarios. Quieting the mind and mentally placing ourselves in the next game, challenging situation, or tough conversation is a powerful tool for growth. Visualization isn't just an exercise; it's a practice that fuels progress and prepares us for what lies ahead.

The brain is a funny and beautifully complicated thing. Have you ever sat on your couch watching a scary movie? Even though you're safe in your own home, you find yourself saying, "Don't open the door, don't open the door," but then, of course, they open it, and you jump. Our brain does not always distinguish between what's real and what is imagined. While this can work against us during a scary movie, it becomes incredibly powerful when you use it to envision your future self. It closes the gap between who you are now and who you aspire to become.

I can't even begin to count how many times I've relied on visualization—it's been a cornerstone of my success. Despite its simplicity and effectiveness, visualization remains one of the most underutilized habits. Yet, it's a defining practice among elite performers. Athletes are perhaps the most well-known for using this technique. They vividly imagine themselves standing on the free throw line, with the game on the line, executing the perfect shot. The most successful individuals in business use the same approach. They envision themselves delivering impactful presentations, securing major deals, and leading their organizations to unparalleled success.

But the true power of visualization extends far beyond picturing yourself nailing the shot, making the big catch, delivering a remarkable keynote, or sealing the deal. Its real strength lies in preparing for the unexpected—mentally rehearsing how you'll respond to setbacks, challenges, and moments of doubt. It's about seeing yourself stumble and recover, miss the shot and take another, or face rejection and keep going. Visualization isn't just about envisioning success; it's about building mental toughness and resilience by practicing how you'll navigate adversity and thrive in the process.

It is about visualizing how we respond to failure. How we respond to failure is one of the foundations for mental toughness and a part of resilience. When we encounter a situation we have not faced before, our brain might say, *I have never been here before,* which can trigger stress. That stress disrupts our focus, and this lapse can make the difference between winning and losing, closing the deal or missing it, or catching a subtle cue that could change the conversation.

By purposefully visualizing both success and failure each morning (with an emphasis on visualizing more success than failure) and focusing on how we would respond to each, we begin to cultivate a resilient mindset. Over time, this practice strengthens our mental toughness, preparing us to stay focused and composed regardless of the outcome. Visualization not only helps us respond to setbacks but also provides clarity about the person we aspire to become.

Dr. Kevin Elko, who owns 30 Super Bowl and NCAA rings and has worked with the Alabama Crimson Tide and other legendary teams, has a powerful phrase, "Believing is seeing." For years, I misunderstood this concept. I thought I had to "see to believe." I felt that unless I could craft a perfect mental picture of success, I couldn't believe in it. This mindset held me back. The truth is that most people struggle to visualize their highest potential because they don't fully believe in it yet. This can be discouraging and, for some, even painful, leading them to give up on visualization altogether. If achieving our goals were as simple as "seeing and believing," we'd all be much further along. But when we can't create that flawless image of our ideal self, we often settle and accept less than we're capable of.

That's why I emphasize the incremental nature of visualization. It's not about creating a perfect image right away. It's about seeing yourself fall short, recover, and ultimately succeed. Picture yourself missing the first shot, regrouping, and nailing the second one. This process builds belief in your ability to grow, adapt, and achieve. Visualization is one of the most powerful tools for fostering this belief and shaping the highest version of yourself.

Many of you might wonder, isn't that the same as seeing? Not at all. The idea of seeing first, then believing, is rooted in the notion that we need to witness results before we can trust in our potential. This is one of the things that limits so many. We think we have to see the results before we develop the confidence in ourselves or others to fully engage. "Believing is seeing" incorporates visualization principles. The only way I can believe it is to visualize, to create a picture so profoundly in my mind of what I want to become that it becomes a part of me. This requires daily consistent effort.

Visualization is a habit that strengthens your focus, confidence, and resilience. It mentally prepares you for success, turning your goals into clear, achievable steps or changing your identity to a new, more powerful one. By incorporating visualization into your daily routine, you align your mindset with your ambitions, making the path to achievement more efficient and more fulfilling. In fact, it's so easy we did it as kids. As kids we believed we could achieve anything, be anyone, and that visualization was a huge part. We would actually see ourselves as superheroes, the Super Bowl-winning quarterback throwing the perfect pass, or the rock star on stage. Then we got away from it. Life gets in the way, and we stop visualizing altogether. Why? Because we didn't see the results.

Before games, I would envision myself calling the game under control, calm, composed, and completely relaxed. I would envision the game on the line, the chaos all around me and, remaining totally and completely focused, envision that game in slow motion. I now incorporate this into my daily life. Because I struggled with this higher version of myself at one point (such as when I was an NFL head coach), I started to envision the best possible version of myself, visualizing myself and my process. I visualized going through the day having great conversations with others, being productive and energetic, being confident, and presenting it with command. As I was able to intentionally bring visualization into my life, what I visualized about myself improved. I was able to envision at a higher level. Doing this daily is not easy, but whether you use vision boards, meditation, affirmations, or, like me, you picture yourself on stage, in front of people. However you tap into that highest version of yourself, what matters is doing it for five to ten minutes daily. You cannot crush it if you cannot visualize it because your brain will fall to its baseline level of programming.

SURROUNDING YOURSELF WITH GAME-CHANGERS

When you think of the New England Patriots, Duke basketball, iconic athletes like Michael Jordan and Kobe Bryant, or powerhouse companies like Amazon, Apple, or Google, one thing stands out: their remarkable ability to consistently perform at an elite level over time. These individuals and organizations didn't just reach the top, they sustained their success and kept raising the bar, redefining excellence in their respective fields.

Such high-level consistency requires more than talent or innovation alone; it demands a culture of excellence, a relentless work ethic, and an unwavering commitment to improvement. Each of these examples reflects a mindset where success is not a one-time event but a repeated, intentional effort to push past benchmarks and redefine what is possible. This type of prolonged success is built on adapting, maintaining focus, and responding to setbacks, setting a standard that others strive to follow but few achieve.

The enduring success of the Patriots, Duke basketball, Michael Jordan, Kobe Bryant, and pioneering companies highlights the power of consistently performing at an exceptional level, not just for a season or a year, but for decades. This sustained excellence becomes a hallmark, inspiring future generations and reshaping industries and expectations.

At the core of this success is the power of the team. Even the greatest of all time, Jordan, Kobe, and Brady, relied on key people to elevate their performance. Jordan had Pippen. Kobe had Shaquille O'Neal. Brady had Gronk. Beyond these iconic partnerships, they were surrounded by a broader team that supported and enabled their success. From personal trainers and mindset coaches to nutritionists and advisors, their teams were essential in creating the foundation for their greatness. True excellence, as they demonstrated, is never achieved alone; it's built alongside others.

Imagine yourself as the general manager or CEO of your own life. Who would you want on your team? Who are your board of advisors? Who are your mentors, coaches, teammates, and support staff? The world's top performers have one thing in common: they build strong teams around themselves because they know they can't achieve greatness alone.

At this point, some of you might hit a mental block, thinking about limitations like not having the right connections or resources. Don't let that stop you. This is your shot to build your dream team.

Start by identifying what you're missing:

- Mentors: Who can guide you with their wisdom and experience?
- Support Staff: What skills do you struggle with or dislike, and who can take those off your plate?
- Board of Advisors: Who are your most trusted sounding boards?
- Growth Leaders: Who is helping you focus on personal or professional development?
- Energy and Wellness: Who ensures you're functioning at your best (like your "sports medicine department")?
- Accountability Partners: Who will hold you to your commitments and keep you on track (your "ethics committee")?

Have fun with this exercise and really think through who belongs on your team and, just as importantly, who doesn't. Remember, no one achieves greatness on their own. Every champion, every top performer, has a team behind them. Now, it's time to build yours!

CLARITY SIMPLIFIES EVERYTHING

Clarity simplifies everything. When we have it, life becomes more straightforward; without it, everything feels harder. Clarity is a vital habit because it lays the foundation for intentionality. There's a distinct difference between purposeful, productive, and fulfilling actions versus taking action just for the sake of doing something. Anyone can take action, but those who approach it with clear intent operate at a higher level. Compare these two statements:

1. "I will be financially free by investing and saving."

2. "I will achieve financial freedom by researching and investing in the best stocks and options. I'll allocate 65 percent of my investments to high-risk, high-reward stocks, while safeguarding 35 percent in lower-yield, stable options. I'll also build an emergency savings account and purchase a life insurance policy for future protection."

The difference is undeniable. Clarity turns vague intentions into a concrete, actionable roadmap. It's one of the most important habits for higher performance and greater success.

This level of intentionality only happens when we have clarity about what we want, who we are, how we want to interact with others, how we want to handle situations or conversations, what type of work makes us excited and fulfilled, and what we want to spend our time on. Now, you can seek and find clarity in tons of other areas, but these are the top categories. By making clarity a habit, you continually define what matters most, directing you in a more meaningful, positive way and allowing you to bring the type of energy to what you are doing. When you have a sense of what is important and what matters to you, decision-making is more straightforward, as is taking unproductive things off your plate. Knowing what matters allows you to delete or hand off the things that do not.

We constantly need clarity, and there is no such thing as having too much of it. At any given time, there will always be a part of your life that requires clarity, and what that clarity looks like will change over time. Your clarity will differ from what you needed three months ago or what you will need three months from now. High performers actively seek clarity, understanding that it's crucial in various areas. This active pursuit of clarity empowers them to control their lives and actions.

Without clarity, there's no direction and no roadmap to follow. Clarity provides that map; we are left uncertain about which path to take without it. Developing clarity is like following a map on a journey. When we commit to the habit of asking ourselves meaningful questions, questions that guide our mind, shape our focus, and set our intentions, we uncover a clear path forward, like a treasure map revealing itself step by step.

Here are some ways to gain clarity:

- **Define your core values.** We all have values. What is at your core? What do you believe in so profoundly that it would move you to take action? What do you value most?
- **Identify what matters.** Ask yourself powerful questions. *What am I passionate about? What about this would make me feel fulfilled about this? What single most important thing should I be focusing on?* Defining your core values can bring relief, as it provides a clear guide for making decisions and living your life.
- **Create space.** Whether in your mind or your physical space, it's hard to work effectively or live thoughtfully in chaos. Create the right environment or find the right environment to gain clarity.
- **Focus on one thing at a time.** In *Getting Things Done* by David Allen, he discusses the concept of "open loops." Open loops are anything you've committed to doing or thinking about but haven't clarified or tracked. Capturing them and gaining clarity around them are the first two steps to closing those open loops. When we split our attention they stay open, and this causes the greatest amount of anxiety and reduces clarity.
- **Block out the noise.** Meditation helps reduce the chatter and helps you become more aware of what you are feeling and what you want.

INTEGRITY: THE CORE OF TRUE EXCELLENCE

Integrity is about far more than just keeping promises—it's about holding yourself to the highest standard, honoring your commitments, and respecting yourself, even when no one else is watching. It's in the small actions, like sticking to the diet you started with your spouse or picking up trash in the locker room when no one else notices. True integrity is rare, and often misunderstood, but it is the foundation of self-trust and confidence. High performers around the world have mastered the ability to own their promises and live by their word. This habit alone fosters incredible confidence and self-belief, a trait that sets them apart.

Football, at its core, is about connection—the connection with your players and the bond formed within the sacred space of the locker room. The locker room is more than just a place to prepare for the game; it's holy ground. It's the one place where the entire team can come together as one, experiencing the raw, unfiltered emotions of victory, defeat, joy, and heartbreak. For anyone who hasn't been in a football locker room, it's hard to describe the magnitude of those emotions, but they are transformative.

Every football game matters. With just 17 regular-season games in the NFL and 18 in the CFL, each win or loss carries immense weight. College and high school seasons are even shorter. Unlike basketball or baseball, where frequent games soften the sting of a loss, football demands year-round preparation for just 60 minutes of action each week. The stakes are higher, and the emotions more intense.

On a team, **integrity is everything.** It builds trust, ensuring players and coaches can rely on each other to be honest, accountable, and committed. It's the glue that binds individuals into a true team. Without it, there's no cohesion—just people going through the motions. Integrity fosters open communication, mutual respect, and a shared commitment to excellence. On the field, it means trusting teammates to execute. Off the field, it creates a culture of accountability, ensuring you do the right things even when no one is watching.

Integrity is the backbone of success. It separates teams that excel from those that crumble under pressure. True leadership comes from living with integrity, inspiring those around you to follow suit. Success built on integrity is lasting and meaningful—without it, any victory is hollow.

After a loss, the locker room feels like a morgue—a heavy silence, faces filled with frustration, anger, and disappointment. Whether dealing with the heartbreak of losing or the euphoria of winning, integrity remains at the core. It means committing to preparation, effort, and resilience—not just saying you'll do it, but showing up and following through. In football, as in life, integrity is putting the team above yourself, even when it's hard, even when you don't feel like it.

In my first year as the head coach at Edmonton, I encountered one of those defining moments where integrity was put to the test. I had to release a player I deeply cared about—someone I truly loved and still do.

This was a person I had shared countless battles with, long meetings solving problems, crushing defeats, and moments of pure joy. Yet, I knew this decision had to be made, even though it wasn't entirely within my control. I also understood that it might cost me my job—and, in the end, it was one of the factors that did. Despite the personal pain it caused, I knew I had to uphold our core beliefs—the shared values that defined us as a team—above all else. To this day, the decision still hurts, but I've come to realize that acting with integrity is rarely easy. It's often the hardest path, but it's also the most necessary if you want to elevate yourself and those around you.

Integrity is a key habit because it pushes you to align your actions with your values, even when it's uncomfortable. Paired with clarity, these habits can be developed, and together, they are foundational to building trust, fostering respect, and striving for excellence.

LOOK FOR INTEGRITY MOMENTS

At the beginning of this section, I mentioned that true integrity is the foundation of self-trust and confidence. Self-trust, which I will delve into more deeply later, is rooted in a core belief: *When things fall apart, I will figure it out.* This kind of trust in yourself isn't developed overnight—it's the result of years of consistently aligning your values with your actions and commitments. Self-trust grows when you follow through on promises, not just to others, but to yourself. It's strengthened when you face challenges and tough decisions head-on, choosing to act with integrity even when it's inconvenient or difficult. This alignment between what you say and what you do creates a powerful sense of confidence and reliability within yourself.

One of my favorite things to witness, both in individuals and teams, is their ability to recognize and act on what I call "integrity moments." These are the everyday opportunities to demonstrate integrity, and they come up far more often than we might think. For example:

- When a waitress accidentally undercharged you, and you choose to pay the correct amount.
- When you pass someone less fortunate and offer a genuine smile or a kind word.

- When you see a piece of trash on the sidewalk, and you take a moment to pick it up, even though it's not your responsibility.
- Or, my personal favorite, cleaning up after your dog during a walk—something that seems so hard for some people yet says so much about accountability and respect for others.

Integrity isn't always about grand gestures. It's built in these small, seemingly insignificant moments, where you have the choice to act in alignment with your values. Each time you choose integrity, you strengthen your self-trust and build confidence, not just in yourself but in how others perceive you. These integrity moments are not just opportunities to do the right thing; they're chances to prove to yourself that you can consistently live up to your own standards, and that's where true self-trust begins. Your challenge is to look for these *integrity moments* and then step into your best self to do what's needed.

A FINAL WORD ON HABITS AS PERFORMANCE STANDARDS

Habits are the seeds of discipline. With strong habits, success becomes attainable because the process remains consistent. Habits provide the structure for growth, but they don't exist in isolation. Behind every habit is something deeper: the performance standards we set for ourselves. Everything comes down to a standard.

Consider this:

- Bill Walsh revolutionized football with his *Standard of Performance*, a meticulous approach that emphasized precision, preparation, and execution at every level.
- Steve Jobs upheld uncompromising standards of design and user experience, creating products that transformed industries and reshaped customer expectations.
- Whether you admire him or not, Jeff Bezos sets relentless standards for innovation and execution speed, driving industries forward at an unparalleled pace.

- Oprah Winfrey defined standards of authenticity, setting the bar for connection and trust in television and media.
- Michael Jordan established a daily standard for competitive excellence, a work ethic that became the benchmark for athletes worldwide.
- Jeff Bezos prioritized customer satisfaction, setting a standard for convenience and reliability that has redefined e-commerce.
- Tiger Woods set a standard for dominance, particularly on Sundays, where his performance under pressure became legendary.

These individuals didn't rise to success solely because of their habits. They became icons in their fields because they first defined their performance standards, the non-negotiable benchmarks they would hold themselves to every single day. Their habits, in turn, were built to meet and exceed those standards. Performance standards are the foundation of everything. They provide clarity, focus, and a framework for growth. They force you to ask what you're willing to demand of yourself every day. The truth is, your standards dictate the habits you develop, the actions you take, and ultimately, the results you achieve.

ACTIONABLE STEPS TO BUILD YOUR STANDARDS

Define your standards. Identify the performance level you must consistently meet to achieve your goals. Be specific.

- If you want to be a top performer in sales, your standard might be to make 50 calls a day and follow up with every lead within 24 hours.
- If you're an athlete, your standard might be to show up to every practice on time and give 100 percent effort in every drill.

Align habits with your standards. Habits are tools that help you meet your standards.

- If your standard is to deliver high-quality work, create a habit of reviewing every project twice before submission.
- If your standard is to stay physically fit, build habits like meal prepping and scheduling workouts in advance.

Evaluate and refine regularly. Standards are not static, and they should evolve as you grow.

- Regularly assess your performance and adjust your standards to push yourself further.

Commit to these standards daily. Greatness isn't achieved occasionally. It's earned through daily commitment.

- Make showing up for your standards non-negotiable.

All of the high achievers mentioned—Walsh, Jobs, Musk, Oprah, Jordan, Bezos, Woods—didn't aim to simply "do well." They aimed to surpass what was considered great. Their performance standards came first, and their habits were built to reinforce those standards.

The lesson here is simple: Define the performance standards you must meet and surpass, and then build habits to ensure you achieve them. Standards guide your discipline, shape your habits, and, ultimately, determine the trajectory of your success.

Courage and resilience are your ticket into the arena, just like an Olympic athlete stepping onto the world stage. Without them, you can't even begin the journey. They are the foundational qualities that prepare you to face challenges, take risks, and push past fear and adversity. But getting into the arena is just the start. To stand on the podium, representing the pinnacle of success, you need more. Just like an Olympian, it takes developing an unstoppable identity and mindset, showing up every day with full engagement, and committing to the key habits that drive performance and progress. These are the qualities that separate competitors from champions, turning effort into excellence.

The next two chapters of *The CRUSH-IT Formula* will show you what you need to reach the top of the podium.

CHAPTER 6
INTERNAL DISCIPLINE

I want you to imagine you are standing on the Olympic medal platform at the Olympics. You are one of the best. The ultimate result after years of preparation, hard work, and sacrifice. You've shown incredible courage, picked yourself up countless times after falling, and built the resilience needed to push through failure after failure. Along the way, you've reshaped your identity, forging a mindset that is unshakable and truly unstoppable. Every day, you've shown up with unwavering passion, energy, and consistency. You've prioritized authentic connections with your coaches, teammates, and support staff, fostering relationships that fuel your growth. You've also developed powerful habits that help you approach everything with great intentionality and razor-sharp focus. Mastery hasn't come alone. It's been supported by a dedicated team of coaches and mentors who have guided you, offering a roadmap to success and pushing you toward your best. But getting to the top of the podium requires something more. It demands the final two aspects of *The CRUSH-IT Formula*: **Internal Discipline** and **Tenacity.** These are the traits that separate those who simply compete from those who conquer. With these last elements of the formula, you'll have everything you need to reach the peak, the top of the platform reserved for Gold medal winners.

Discipline is a word that often carries a weighty, almost negative connotation. For many, it feels like a "dirty word," something associated with restriction, rigidity, or even guilt. When I first reflected on the role of discipline in my own life, my thoughts immediately turned self-critical. *This is where I lack discipline. I wish I were more disciplined here. Have I ever truly been disciplined enough? How can I possibly teach others about discipline when I haven't mastered it myself?*

Discipline, for so many of us, has a way of highlighting our perceived shortcomings. It stirs up feelings of inadequacy, a sense that we don't have enough of it or that we've fallen short in certain areas. But as I dug deeper and began reflecting on the pivotal moments of my life, something surprising happened. I started to see the countless times I *did* rely on discipline, not as a rigid constraint, but as a steady guide that helped me grow, overcome challenges, and achieve significant milestones.

In these moments, discipline wasn't about perfection or self-criticism. It was about consistency, focus, and showing up even when it was hard. It was the quiet force behind the scenes that allowed me to stay on course, even in the face of setbacks. What I realized was this: discipline doesn't have to be a burden or a source of guilt. Instead, it can be an empowering tool that fuels growth, supports intentional action, and helps us achieve what matters most.

Discipline, at its core, demands mental toughness above all else. It's a concept that's difficult to fully grasp or embody, yet we can recognize it in certain individuals. We see it in athletes competing on the field or during the Olympics, and in other relentless, high-achieving individuals who consistently accomplish more than most. Mental toughness and discipline often go hand in hand, and we admire those who seem to have it in abundance. For many of us, they represent qualities we aspire to develop, as we think, *I wish I had more of that.*

When I think of mental toughness, names like Michael Jordan, Serena Williams, Tom Brady, and Simone Biles immediately come to mind. These athletes embody the psychological resilience and strength that allow them to persevere, stay focused, and perform at their best under pressure, adversity, or stress. Mental toughness isn't just about physical ability; it's about maintaining a positive mindset, staying motivated, and pushing through challenges, even in the face of setbacks or disappointment. I've certainly faced my share of those moments, but

I've come to realize that mental toughness is essential for building discipline.

In a seminal study, researchers Graham Jones, Sheldon Hanton, and Declan Connaughton defined mental toughness as "an athlete's ability to outperform their competitors in managing demands and demonstrating consistency, drive, focus, confidence, and control under pressure." They found that mental toughness is not only an innate quality but also something that can be developed over time. This means that even if someone doesn't appear to be "born with it," they can absolutely cultivate it through deliberate effort and practice. What I love about this definition is its emphasis on growth. Mental toughness isn't just a gift, it's a skillset, and like any skill, it can be learned, refined, and mastered over time.

When we think of a mentally tough individual, we picture someone with determination, inner strength, and confidence. They stay composed under pressure and are able to manage their emotions effectively, no matter the circumstances. But mental toughness isn't just about enduring hardship, it's about thriving in difficult moments, using adversity as fuel for growth and transformation. Mental toughness is rooted in the process, and that's where discipline comes into play. It's about intentional, consistent actions that push you through challenges, discomfort, boredom, and even pain. Discipline and mental toughness are deeply interconnected. Discipline demands mental toughness to stay consistent, while mental toughness is built through the practice of discipline. Many people mistakenly think it's about motivation, but motivation is fleeting—it can only take you so far. Discipline, on the other hand, is the driver. It's what allows you to keep going when every part of your body and mind is screaming at you to stop. Discipline creates the resilience to endure and the strength to thrive, even in the toughest moments.

I like to break down discipline into three distinct aspects, much like the principles of energy: physical discipline, mental discipline, and emotional discipline. Similar to how energy can vary from person to person, some aspects of discipline come more naturally to us than others. For some, physical discipline is the biggest challenge, staying consistent with workouts, pushing through physical discomfort, and maintaining a routine can feel like an uphill battle. For others, the struggle lies in mental discipline, whether it's staying focused, keeping a positive attitude, maintaining concentration, or eliminating self-defeating thoughts. And for many, the greatest difficulty is emotional discipline, managing feelings, staying composed under pressure, and not letting emotions dictate decisions. Understanding these three aspects allows us to pinpoint where we need to grow and focus our efforts to build a balanced, disciplined life.

PHYSICAL DISCIPLINE: THE CORE DISCIPLINE

Let us start with physical discipline. To me, this is a prerequisite. Some may disagree, but you must push yourself physically to establish discipline for several reasons. Number one, it builds consistency. Physical discipline, like exercising regularly, requires you to develop consistency regardless of mood or level of motivation. This consistency shows up in other areas of your life and strengthens your ability to stick with your commitments. Number two, it builds mental resilience by forcing you to push through physical discomfort or fatigue and teaches you to go further when you do not want to or feel like you cannot. Doing so increases your ability to be persistent in other areas. Unlike mental and emotional discipline, physical discipline gives you immediate feedback on your progress or lack thereof. You cannot hide when it comes to the progress that your "physical" discipline reveals. Physical discipline helps regulate your emotions and provides a strong foundation for self-control. When you see progress physically, it enables you to regulate your impulses in other areas. You become less likely to succumb to temptations, miss a workout, skip a day, or go for that bag of chips when you know better. Doing so reinforces your discipline, seeping into other areas of your life.

When you develop this kind of self-discipline, something else happens: You create a deeper level of self-trust. Self-trust, built up over time, produces a different benefit. When life throws you a curveball, and it will, you develop an unshakeable belief that you will figure things out. In Chapter Three, we discussed the importance of choices, particularly how good choices impact your energy. The more energy you have, the more disciplined you can be, especially when it applies to mental discipline. Discipline is about choices. Setting up your environment is vital to helping you make good choices and preventing the derailment of your discipline.

MENTAL DISCIPLINE: MAINTAINING FOCUS AMID DISTRACTIONS

This is the ability to consistently manage your thoughts, maintain focus, and stay in control of your mindset, no matter the distractions, challenges, or feelings that come your way. It also involves staying committed as motivation wanes. A key part of this is the capacity to block out distractions and channel intense focus when it matters most.

When I think of mental discipline, Hall of Fame quarterback Peyton Manning immediately comes to mind. His extraordinary ability to analyze everything happening on the field, focus with pinpoint precision on the defense's moves, and adjust the play to give his team the best possible advantage was truly unmatched. He simply never allowed himself to get distracted by the unimportant, maintaining an unwavering focus on what truly mattered. Whether it was analyzing the defense, executing the game plan, or leading his team under immense pressure, he had the mental discipline to block out anything that didn't contribute to the goal at hand. This ability to tune out noise—both external distractions and internal doubts—was a key part of what set him apart as a leader and a competitor. Physically, Peyton Manning was considered to have one of the weakest arms of any starting quarterback, yet he more than made up for it with his knowledge of the game. He, like many highly successful people, was relentless in the face of adversity.

When the pressure is on, I pay close attention to how someone talks to themselves and where their mindset is. Does their chest rise with confidence, or do they look down after a critical moment? What do their eyes reveal? Are they locked in with laser focus, or do they carry a flicker of doubt?

How well do you block out distractions when the stakes rise? Do you feel the pressure, the stress of the moment, or can you focus past that and lock into the task at hand? The last area I look for when assessing a person's mental discipline is their ability to make decisions when the heat is on. Do you see someone adjust their decision-making process and do something out of the ordinary? Do you see them and go,

"What are they thinking?" The ability to maintain mental discipline in these moments is paramount and ties into our decision-making under pressure.

EMOTIONAL DISCIPLINE: STAYING NEUTRAL UNDER PRESSURE

Discipline, in psychological terms, relates to emotional discipline or the art of acknowledging, understanding, and managing your feelings and emotions in a healthy and constructive way. In essence, you have the power to choose how you feel. Feelings, as we know, are powerful forces. If left unchecked, they can easily overwhelm us, sometimes without us even realizing it. They don't just affect our moods, they shape the quality of our thoughts and heavily influence the decisions we make. Leadership expert Charles Manz contends that we can control our emotions and direct them into constructive channels. He calls the ability to choose how we feel "emotional discipline." In his book *Emotional Discipline: The Power to Choose How You Feel*, Manz focuses on our ability to use emotions to work for us and use their energy in positive ways.

I wasn't very good at this when I was younger, especially when I first started out. I've always been an emotional person, and while that can be a strength, it didn't always serve me positively. Looking back, I now firmly believe that my lack of emotional discipline was closely tied to my identity, or rather, the identity I felt I needed to prove. There was this constant pressure to show that I belonged, and that mindset kept me in a heightened emotional state. When things were going well, my emotions weren't an issue, but when adversity struck, it was a different story. That's when the cracks started to show. A lack of emotional discipline reveals itself in many ways: difficulty managing stress, strained relationships, impulsive decisions, procrastination, avoidance, negativity, and ineffective communication. It can also lead to unresolved conflicts, which only worsen over time. My solution was to work harder. The *right* solution was to do the work to figure out what was triggering me, and then develop sound strategies to remain neutral. Remaining neutral is an easy concept to understand but more difficult to employ.

The key is developing awareness of the specific areas where you lack emotional discipline. It's not enough to simply say, "I need to be more disciplined." That's far too vague and overly simplistic. Building emotional discipline starts by removing negativity from your thinking. As Trevor Mowad writes in his books, it takes what it takes, but thinking positively isn't enough. Moawad emphasizes that positive thinking alone isn't sufficient for achieving success. He introduces the concept of "neutral thinking," which involves accepting the reality of past events without judgment and focusing on the present moment to determine the next best steps. Moawad argues that while positive thinking is often linked to specific outcomes, neutral thinking centers on present actions, enabling individuals to manage challenges more effectively. Moawad also highlights the detrimental impact of negative thinking, noting that it can significantly hinder performance and decision-making. He points out that negative thoughts are more powerful than positive ones and that verbalizing negative thoughts can further amplify their impact. Research shows that positive thinking is not as effective as eliminating negative thinking. We can't always be positive, but we can always be less negative with our thoughts and our self-talk.

I often talk with my clients and the athletes I train about recognizing indicators. By the time you notice a trigger, it's already too late, but there are always warning signs, or red flags that appear before we reach that point. Reflect on the moments where you responded in ways you later regretted, and you'll often find there were indicators signaling you were on the verge of being emotionally compromised. High-performing individuals don't allow themselves to reach that breaking point. One of the ways they maintain emotional discipline is by recognizing those indicators well in advance, often from a mile away, and taking intentional action to stay in control.

What helped me gain greater control in this area was simple, yet it had quite an impact. I simply quit verbalizing my doubt and reasons why I couldn't do something out loud or to others. I made a conscious effort to stop giving power to disempowering thoughts by speaking them aloud. It wasn't overnight, and at first, it took a while to catch it when I did. Over time, I improved. It didn't mean the thoughts didn't occasionally show up, I just didn't put them into words. So what did I do when I caught those disempowering thoughts or feelings? I trained myself to mentally erase them. Ed Mylett talks about a similar practice.

He visualizes himself scribbling over the doubt on a blackboard or piece of paper until it completely disappears. I adopted the same approach, picturing myself scratching out the negative thought in my mind, refusing to let it take hold, and actually forcing myself, at first, to replace it with a positive thought or statement. This, in and of itself, took discipline. And yet, over time, it helped me break the cycle of reinforcing doubt and allowed me to regain control over my mindset and self-talk.

Emotional discipline is essential, especially if you aspire to reach your highest level of success. It's equally crucial as a leader, where composure and control can define your impact and influence.

CULTIVATING THE RIGHT APPROACH AND MINDSET AROUND DISCIPLINE

If you're serious about building discipline, it starts with the right mindset and a willingness to accept where you currently stand. The truth is, you are where you are today because of your level of discipline, or lack of it. For most people, the choices they've made, both big and small, have been shaped by a lack of consistent discipline.

But here's the reality: discipline is 100 percent within your control. How much of it you develop is entirely up to you. And yet, so many of us struggle with it. Why? Because we often view discipline as something elusive, as if it's a trait some people are simply born with. We say things like, "I wish I had more discipline," or "I'm just not a disciplined person." But that perspective needs to shift. Discipline isn't some rare, magical quality—it's a skill. And like any skill, it can be developed and strengthened over time. The choice is yours: how much discipline do you truly want in your life? There is no right or wrong answer—only what's right for you.

Start by asking yourself these three key questions:

1. What level of discipline do I currently have in different areas of my life?
2. What have been the consequences of not having enough discipline in [fill in the blank] area of my life? Be honest here.

3. What mindset do I need to develop to strengthen my discipline?

Your perspective around discipline shapes everything. How you perceive it will determine whether you embrace it or resist it. Ask yourself if you see discipline as a necessary evil, a best friend, or something like eating kale—unpleasant but beneficial, Sorry, kale lovers!

- **Discipline as a necessary evil.** If you see it as a burden or something you have to do, it will always feel like a struggle. You will naturally approach it with some level of resistance, and you'll look for shortcuts and practice only when it's a must. Inconsistency in your levels of discipline will result.
- **Discipline as a best friend.** Now, when discipline is seen as a trusted ally, things change. Instead of resistance, you embrace it and understand it as a key to unlocking your potential. Shifting your mindset from discipline being something to avoid, to something you can rely on, provides clarity and confidence that fuels success.
- **Discipline as kale (unpleasant but beneficial).** This mindset sits in the middle. You acknowledge that discipline may not always feel good and won't be easy, but you understand its value. This builds consistency, and embracing temporary discomfort will lead to long-term rewards.

REFRAMING YOUR MINDSET: DISCIPLINE AND SELF-RESPECT

The key is to redefine discipline as a choice rather than an obligation. Instead of thinking, *I have to be disciplined,* shift your mindset to *I get to be disciplined.* Discipline is not a restriction, it's a form of self-respect, a commitment to your future self. So, how do you currently view discipline? And, more importantly, how do you want to see it moving forward? Choosing to see discipline as your best friend rather than a necessary evil will determine how consistently you apply it in your life.

Cutting the "Shoulds"

We've all heard the phrase "cut the shit." But if you want more discipline, it's time to cut the "shoulds." I *should* have worked out more. I *should* have eaten better. I *should* have listened more, been more present, or shown more love. Sound familiar? We all have our own list of shoulds. But "should" is just another way of avoiding responsibility. Take a hard look at all the areas of your life where you find yourself saying *I should*. Then, recognize the power of choice that you have. *Can I live with this "should" staying as it is?* If the answer is yes, move on. But if the answer is anything less than a resounding yes, then ask yourself, *Do I want to live with the pain of discipline* or *the pain of regret?* That choice is yours, always. And choices are the real game-changer.

Making This Practical

How do you actually apply this? Start by tracking your "shoulds" each day. Keep a mental (or written) note of every time you catch yourself saying, "I should have..." At the end of the day, take a few minutes to reflect on how often it happened. While tracking your shoulds is important, being truthful with yourself is essential. The goal isn't just to count them—it's to prevent the ultimate regret: the big "should" you look back on later in life when it's too late to change course. Discipline starts with cutting the shoulds and replacing them with action. The sooner you do, the fewer regrets you'll have.

Get Up Early—Get the First First Down

Yes, get up early. Discipline starts the moment you get out of bed. I did it for over 22 years in football, and I still do it today. Some days—most days—it sucks. It's not easy. There are mornings when every fiber of my body fights against it. But I do it anyway for two key reasons. First, it creates an immediate win. Starting strong sets the tone for everything that follows. Just like in football, where we script the first fifteen to twenty plays to ensure a strong start, I approach my mornings the same way. The goal? Get that *first* first down. Waking up early is my first victory of the day, the momentum builder that carries me forward.

Second, it reinforces discipline, belief, and confidence. By consistently doing what's hard, I strengthen my ability to push through in other areas of life. It's a ripple effect—one strong habit leads to another, creating momentum that fuels my success. And over time, I've come to appreciate the quiet and stillness of early mornings. It's when I get the most done, free from distractions, fully in control of how my day begins.

Like elite performers, I, too, have a morning routine that I follow. The key is finding what works for you, but I think some key components exist. Connecting to your burn, which we will discuss below, is a must, along with hydrating. A meditation or focus on gratitude helps set the day for being centered, and I love to start the day with a workout and then some reading. Lastly, I shift into my day and finish with visualizations. That is my order and my method. I encourage you to figure out what works for you.

Access Your Burn

This concept of "the burn" comes from Ben Newman, a friend and fellow coach who is considered one of the best performance coaches in the world. He is also an incredible human being. Ben first taught me the concept of the burn or reminded me of my burn, even though I had never thought of it that way. To create more discipline in your life, you must tap into something inside yourself that is more powerful than your purpose or why. It is something that allows you to do the difficult things and emerge victorious. It is so deep that, as Ben says, "It ignites your why and purpose." I am grateful for Ben, who helped me remember what allowed me to do the hard stuff before.

As you may remember, my dad passed away when I was just six months old. He was only 26. I've often wondered—what would he do if he had *one more day*? That thought has stayed with me, and now, every morning when I wake up, I tap into it. The moment my eyes open, my first thought is, *One more day*. What would my dad do if he had just one more? He wouldn't let an alarm clock or a pillow defeat him. He wouldn't put off a phone call out of fear or hesitation. He wouldn't skip a workout because he was sore or tired. And he wouldn't miss an opportunity to tell someone he loved them. This mindset, *one more day*, is what gets me out of bed every morning. It pushes me forward. It reminds me to make the most of every moment because we never know how many we have left. It's what Ben would call "my burn."

Whatever you call your burn—heart fuel, inner passion, core foundation, or your driving force—it doesn't matter. What matters is you tap into it and use it every single day. Here's an important distinction: this isn't necessarily the same as your why or your purpose. Your *why* might be your family, your wife, and your kids. Your *purpose* might be helping others become the highest version of themselves. While both are meaningful, they may not be enough to get you out of bed at 5 a.m. or push you through the toughest challenges.

To consistently show up and do the hard things, you need to access that *burn*, that deep, personal drive that fuels you beyond motivation. It's not just about knowing your why, it's about finding what ignites you to take action every single day, especially when it's uncomfortable.

THE ROCK WALL: WHERE DISCIPLINE IS FORGED

As much as I wanted to be the next Brett Favre, my football career ended before it even started. I had surgery on my stomach when I was in high school, and I was told I would not be able to play contact sports for a "long time," whatever that meant. With football off the table, I picked up a tennis racket and quickly realized I had a natural talent for the game. But excelling at tennis required resources, and we didn't have many. My stepdad, who raised me alongside my mom, was a firefighter, and my mom worked at a bank. We couldn't afford private lessons or expensive training facilities. So, I improvised.

I started practicing on our sloped driveway, hitting balls against our white garage door. That experiment lasted only two days until my dad came home and saw the garage door covered in dirt marks. With that option off-limits, I turned to the only thing left, the big rock wall in our backyard. While we lacked material resources, I had that wall, and it became my training ground.

But this wasn't just any rock wall. It was a 12-foot-high structure made of cement and large, uneven boulders. I spent countless hours in that backyard, pounding a tennis ball against it. The surface was unpredictable, far from the flat, controlled rebound of a proper tennis court. The ball ricocheted wildly, forcing me to adjust constantly. Over time, I discovered a few precise spots on the wall where the ball would bounce back consistently—but only if I hit them just right. So, I trained myself to focus intensely, aiming for those exact points over and over again. I spent hours pounding the rock wall.

That's when I truly felt what discipline was. Repetition. Focus. Commitment. That rock wall didn't just sharpen my tennis skills; it became the place where I forged the habits that would shape my future. The process of developing discipline, or any skill, often requires looking back at moments in our lives when we demonstrated it at a high level. When were you at your most disciplined? Your most courageous? Your most energized? By reflecting on those moments, we remind ourselves that we already have the ability, we just need to access it again. I call this the rock wall.

What was your rock wall? What challenge, habit, or routine shaped your discipline? We all have something, something we returned to over and over, that strengthened our resilience and commitment. Think back to your own rock wall, reflect on it, and tap into the discipline it helped you build. For me, that rock wall was just the beginning. Since then, discipline has been a constant.

SHOWING UP WHEN IT'S THE HARDEST

That repeated practice of discipline has been the driving force behind my achievements. I came to fully understand this during my time at Northwestern Mutual in 2020, in the midst of the COVID-19 pandemic. Under the guidance of Tom Stewart and Chantal Bonneau, I began to see discipline from a different perspective. It's easy to put in extra hours, wake up early, and stay late when you're passionate about something, when the work itself fuels you. That was me with football. I never had to force myself to show up because I loved it. But true discipline is tested when you're doing something that doesn't excite you in the same way. It's in those moments, when the spark isn't there, when the work feels monotonous, and when the results aren't immediate, that discipline becomes the deciding factor.

During COVID, I found myself in unfamiliar territory, transitioning into the world of financial investments, an industry I knew nothing about. In August 2020, I packed up my life, drove my wife and daughter north to Canada, then drove across the country alone, in the middle of a pandemic, to start a new career at Northwestern Mutual. Everything about this move was outside my comfort zone. Unlike football, when I had spent years developing my skills and instincts, I was now stepping into a field where I was starting from scratch. I had no background in financial advising, no established expertise, and no built-in passion to carry me through.

Stepping into an entirely new industry forced me to develop a different kind of discipline, the kind that isn't fueled by passion but by commitment. I didn't have the same internal fire that football gave me, but I still had a responsibility—to myself, to my family, and to the vision I had for my future. I had to show up, learn, and prove to myself that I could excel in something completely foreign.

I've always sought out mentors and was fortunate to have Tom Stewart take me under his wing. He saw something in me and made a deep investment in my growth. The first thing he noticed? I was always in the office before him, and he was an early riser. At 6 a.m., he'd walk in to find me sitting at my desk, the only light in the office glowing in the early morning darkness. I wasn't passionate about the work, but I was committed—committed to showing up, making the calls, handling rejection, and continuously finding ways to improve. I had days where I didn't want to be there, where the rejection felt relentless, and where I questioned whether I had made the right decision. But I kept going. Not because I loved it, but because I had a clear vision for myself and my family, and I refused to let discomfort or unfamiliarity derail me.

Through my time at Northwestern Mutual, I came to a powerful realization: discipline has always been one of my greatest strengths, even when I've doubted it. That so-called "dirty word," the one so many people resist, isn't a burden. It's a powerful ally. It's what carried me through my football days, through my transition into a completely new industry, and through the countless challenges I've faced along the way. And more importantly, it's the foundation of self-trust. Because when you prove to yourself, day after day, that you can show up and do the work, even when it's hard, you build a level of trust in yourself that no rejection or challenge can shake.

FOCUS ON THINGS THAT DEVELOP SELF-TRUST

The formula is simple: the more discipline we have, the more confidence we build. That's an easy connection to make. But the real magic lies in developing self-trust. While discipline fosters self-trust, it's self-trust that enables us to thrive in the face of adversity. How is this tied to discipline? When you repeatedly show up, especially in the moments when you don't want to, when staying in bed feels easier, when the path of least resistance calls, you cultivate discipline. Pushing forward in these moments strengthens self-trust. By consistently honoring your commitments to yourself, you prove that you can rely on your own actions. Over time, this deepens your belief that you will do what you say you will.

When self-trust becomes ingrained in your identity, when it's simply who you are, you reach a new level of resilience. In life's toughest moments, you instinctively draw upon that hard-earned confidence, knowing you will find a way forward. You trust yourself not because of blind optimism, but because, time and time again, you have done the difficult things that forged that belief. Here are some easy things to help build your self-trust:

- **Keep the small promises.** There is an over-emphasis on doing the big things right. I always looked for players that did the small things right. Did they keep the small promises they made to me and to themselves, or did they discount them? In building self-trust, the little things matter more than the big things. They add up.
- **Set and hold personal boundaries.** This means saying "no" more often. One of the biggest problems high achievers have is they say yes to everything. You cannot be everything to everybody. In fact, what actually holds many of my clients back is the fact that they haven't learned how to say no. I used this with one client when I first began coaching. I have given this a name since then: The 3-Day Rule. This approach helps you make confident decisions and build self-trust by giving yourself three days before

committing to or rejecting something you have been asked to undertake. Here's how it works:

Day 1: Say No/Gut Check: When presented with an opportunity (like serving on a board of directors), resist the urge to give an immediate yes. Instead, say no—at least in your mind. You might have to say you'll think about it. Then, check in with yourself. How does it feel in your body? Does it excite you or bring hesitation?

Day 2: The Logic Test: Write down every possibility why it might be a yes. Analyze the decision from a rational perspective. Does it align with your values, goals, and priorities? Would saying yes create unnecessary stress, or does it serve your long-term growth?

Day 3: The Confident Choice: If your gut and logic both point in the same direction, trust yourself and commit. If doubt lingers, it's likely a no. This intentional pause helps prevent over-committing and builds confidence in your decisions.

By consistently using The 3-Day Rule, you'll strengthen self-trust, avoid impulsive choices, and learn to stand by your decisions with confidence.

- **Practice self-accountability.** Everyone talks about needing an accountability partner. Often, this is simply another excuse. It's important to conduct regular self-check in on what you're doing well and what you're not—where you failed to honor commitments to yourself and others. The key is to do this without self-judgment. I do this as a weekly practice. At first, you'll likely notice multiple times where you fell short. I almost stopped doing it because it made me feel bad about myself. But I stayed the course, and now it's one of the most important self-aligning tools I use.

FALL IN LOVE WITH THE FUNDAMENTALS

Discipline is about embracing the things you need to do, even when they feel repetitive or mundane. It means committing to the fundamentals again and again, without shortcuts. It means falling in love with the fundamentals.

In his book *Raise Your Game*, Alan Stein Jr. shares an insightful story about Kobe Bryant's unwavering commitment to the basics. In 2007, Nike invited Alan to the inaugural Kobe Bryant Skills Academy in Los Angeles, bringing together top high school and college players for an intensive three-day camp. Alan, eager to observe Kobe's renowned training regimen, asked if he could watch one of his workouts. Kobe agreed, mentioning he would start at 4 a.m.

Determined to impress, Alan arrived at the gym by 3:30 a.m., only to find the lights already on and Kobe in a full sweat, having been there for some time. For the next 45 minutes, Alan watched as Kobe meticulously performed basic drills—ball-handling, footwork, and fundamental offensive moves. Struck by the simplicity of the exercises, Alan later asked Kobe why he, as the best player in the world, focused so intently on the basics.

Kobe's response was profound: "Why do you think I'm the best player in the game? Because I never get bored with the basics." This encounter underscored the importance of discipline and a relentless commitment to mastering the fundamentals. Kobe's dedication to the basics was a cornerstone of his success, emphasizing that true excellence comes from a deep appreciation and mastery of foundational skills.

The fundamentals are things that you have to do better than anyone else. And the fundamentals do not change, whether you're a peewee football player at five years old, a high school star at 15, a first-time Pro Bowl selection at 25, a Super Bowl champion at 35, or the G.O.A.T. (Greatest of All Time), Tom Brady, at 45. Too many young players move away from the basics, thinking, *I'm already good at that,* and instead focus on other things. But if you look at the best in any sport, they excel because they have mastered the fundamentals to an elite level. This principle applies beyond sports. In business, success comes down to identifying and consistently executing your company's fundamentals

—the daily actions that drive long-term results. Whether in sports or business, mastery of the basics is what separates the best from the rest.

MAKING CHANGES THAT STICK: BECOME A TWO-PERCENTER

We've all been there. *I want to change, but I keep slipping back into old habits. I start strong, stay disciplined for a while, but eventually fall off.* You're not alone. Developing discipline means changing your behaviors, and that's not easy. Real change doesn't happen overnight, it follows a process. When people ask how to build lasting discipline, I point to the six stages of behavioral change, a proven framework for making deep, meaningful transformations.

> **Stage 1: Recognizing the need for change.**
> Most people begin in denial or unawareness. They either don't recognize the need for change or convince themselves they're fine as they are. You hear it in their self-talk: *I don't need more discipline, I'm only a little overweight, I'll make up for it later.* Moving forward requires acknowledging reality. No one is coming to save you or do the work for you. And until you fully accept this, you're stuck in this stage.
>
> **Stage 2: Contemplation. Shifting internally.**
> Once awareness sets in, you start to reflect and ask deeper questions. *Why am I not getting the results I want? Where am I falling short? What habits or behaviors do I need to change?* This is progress. You are now thinking about making the changes.
>
> **Stage 3: Preparation.**
> You begin creating a plan for success. You develop a roadmap and identify the obstacles, challenges, and distractions that could come up. You are prioritizing and outlining exactly what needs to be done for success to occur. However, most people never make it past this stage. Out of 100 people who set a goal, 70 will stay stuck in planning mode, never taking real action. As I mentioned earlier on, the start is the stop.

Stage 4: Action.
This is where change actually happens. Action is the separator between those who dream and those who do. It's getting up at 5 a.m. to work out, writing that book, or making that difficult decision. However, action alone isn't enough. The real test comes when you face your first major challenge. Many people retreat to their comfort zones at this point. This is why 90 percent of people quit after starting.

Stage 5: Momentum and consistency.
Momentum is the game-changer. In football, a big play can ignite a comeback and breathe life back into a team. In life, consistent discipline builds unstoppable momentum. But momentum isn't just about progress; it's about pushing forward even when motivation fades. The biggest mistake people make? They stop when they feel good. For many people that get to this stage, when they hit two or three setbacks, they falter. Out of the final 10, eight give up, shutting down their business, abandoning their goals, or retreating to comfort, leaving two individuals.

Stage 6: Mastery. Discipline equals freedom.
True discipline isn't about short-term wins. It means having a process that becomes a way of life. When this happens, you experience the ultimate freedom. Freedom from fear and limiting beliefs, freedom from inconsistency and self-doubt, and freedom to take on any challenges with confidence. Only two out of 100 make it to this level.

That's why it's called the two percent rule.

ELIMINATING WEAKNESS AND OPTIMIZING PERFORMANCE

These six stages cultivate a mindset of self-accountability, one that refuses to tolerate weakness or excuses. At one of the places I coached, we had t-shirts that read: *"Pain is only weakness leaving the body."* It was a powerful reminder. Of course, I'm not talking about the pain from life-altering illnesses. That's a different kind of struggle. I'm referring to the chosen pain of pushing yourself, of embracing discomfort in a workout, in training, or in any difficult pursuit. When we lean into that pain, it truly is weakness leaving the body.

I urge you to ask yourself where you might be tolerating weakness. Where are you giving in to short-term gratification? Discipline is the tool that eliminates weakness—one habit, decision, and action at a time. Over time, it refines you, shaping you into a stronger, more resilient version of yourself.

AVOIDING DEPLETION

One of the key understandings around the science of discipline is the concept of *ego depletion*. Ego depletion is the idea that self-control or willpower draws upon finite mental resources, which can become exhausted when used excessively. This is especially true when we've had to exert discipline throughout the day when we make tough decisions, resist temptations, or maintain focus under stress. When our self-control becomes fatigued, much like a muscle after an intense workout, it weakens and becomes harder to use. This is why discipline often fades as the day progresses. The key to maintaining self-discipline is to minimize the number of ego-depleting situations we put ourselves in daily, so we don't drain our mental reserves unnecessarily.

Everything in peak performance is about being at max capacity when it matters most. In football, for example, we scheduled our final practice at least 48 hours before a game to allow for maximum recovery, ensuring that players were at full strength come kickoff. The same principle applies to self-discipline in everyday life. If you burn through your willpower early in the day, you'll find yourself depleted by evening. And that's when discipline often matters most, when you're tempted to skip a workout, indulge in junk food, or pour that extra glass of wine. To preserve discipline when it counts, you must structure your environment to reduce decision fatigue. Remove temptations, automate routine choices, and set up systems that eliminate unnecessary decision-making in areas where you struggle. By doing this, you save your self-control for the moments that truly matter.

DISCIPLINE: MASTERING YOUR PROCESS

Discipline is your most reliable ally. If you embrace it, it will always be there for you. But discipline isn't just about enduring hardship—it's about mastering your process. This is something we emphasize heavily in football: process over outcome. Discipline isn't about winning or losing—it's about creating a system you can control and trust. In my years of coaching, we had a process for everything, from game-planning and play-calling to teaching, reviewing film, coaching on the field, and making halftime adjustments. As you know from earlier, we even had a structured process for how we built the call sheet. These systems were about more than routines; they were designed to keep our focus and discipline on the process, not the outcome. By trusting the process, we eliminated distractions, made better decisions under pressure, and positioned ourselves for success one deliberate step at a time.

The best teams and individuals don't rely on luck or motivation. They trust their preparation, stick to their routines, and execute with precision. When you focus on your process, rather than obsessing over results, anxiety decreases because you trust in your preparation, self-judgment fades because you recognize success isn't defined by a single win or loss, and freedom grows because you're no longer at the mercy of external circumstances.

MENTAL TOUGHNESS AND THE POWER OF MEDITATION

One of the greatest lessons from sports is that you can't always control the outcome, but you can control your response. Fifty percent of teams lose every week, yet the best athletes don't dwell on failure. They refine their process, adjust, and move forward. However, mental toughness is as much about pushing through challenges as it is about recognizing emotions, identifying distractions, and staying focused despite adversity. Meditation plays a key role in this. It has been proven to enhance mental toughness by strengthening focus, emotional regulation, and resilience. By practicing meditation, individuals can better understand their impulses and develop the ability to manage them effectively, leading to improved self-control and more disciplined behavior. Meditation has been determined to be the number one driver of high performance, and it is crucial in developing mental toughness and discipline.

THE GAME PLAN: OPTIMIZING YOUR DAY LIKE A HIGH PERFORMER

The world's highest achievers game plan every day, just like football coaches plan for a big game. If you've ever been in a football strategy meeting, you know how intense it is. Every minute is used to organize, challenge, adjust, and prepare for every possible scenario. By the end, we feel like we've run a marathon, but we walk away with a clear plan of attack. This same level of intentionality and structure applies to life and to your plan for developing more discipline.. The most successful people in the world start early, refine their plan, and optimize their schedule. I love this mindset so much that even my six-year-old asks me every morning, "Daddy, what's the game plan?" It's a simple but powerful question. What's your game plan today? Because in the end, success isn't random.

Take your own discipline to the next level. Access the Daily Discipline Checklist here.

SCAN THE QR CODE:

CHAPTER 7
TENACITY

I sat outside watching my six-year-old daughter trying to do her first chin-up. I saw this look of frustration and anger. Still, more importantly, I saw under that look, under those eyes, a look of determination, perseverance, and an overwhelming desire to prove me wrong.

We were working through these Ninja Warrior kids tools, these incredible tools that help build and develop kids' ability to do difficult things. If you have ever watched the show Ninja Warrior, you probably felt inspired by kids pushing themselves to overcome difficult challenges. But while watching is one thing, being in a moment of struggle is another. We had been working on her first chin-up—just one—which, for a six-year-old, is no small feat.

After 20 minutes of trying, I could see the fatigue setting in. Her fingers were sore, her arms were trembling, and I could tell doubt was creeping in. Her body was telling her she couldn't do it, but there was something else in her eyes: a battle between quitting and pushing forward. As we went back and forth, I offered a way out: "Let's go inside and rest for a bit—it's 105 degrees out." But at that moment, the real test wasn't physical—it was mental. Would she give in, or would she fight for it?

She shook her head, and I said, "I'm proud of you. You gave it your best effort today. Maybe we can't do it today. Perhaps we are still not ready. Period." Period is such a powerful word, but more on that later. I continued, "Sweetheart, we can return here later this evening and try again."

A resounding shake of the head, no. My daughter was determined to stay out there, even if it meant staying until midnight. I know this because I asked her, "Are we really going to stay out here until midnight?" She didn't say a word. She just looked at me the look of a stone-cold killer and gave a single, tenacious nod.

TENACITY

We've all heard the word **Tenacity,** but what does it actually look like in action? Let's define it. Having tenacity means being persistent, determined, and unwilling to give up. It's the mindset of someone who refuses to be swayed by obstacles or challenges. Tenacity isn't just about persistence, it also embodies resilience, focus, patience, endurance, and self-discipline. It's the ability to push forward when others quit, to keep going when things get tough, and to stay committed long after motivation fades. At its core, tenacity means not letting go, not giving up, and outlasting the rest. It's not something you're simply born with. It's something you develop through constant effort and relentless commitment. When I think of truly tenacious people, I think of those who don't just try hard but those who keep going long after everyone else has stopped.

Who is the most tenacious person you know? Is it you? Tenacity is what allows you to push through exhaustion, frustration, and setbacks. It's what separates those who quit from those who persist. Tenacity is the fire that keeps burning even when motivation fades. It's the voice that says, *I will not stop until I succeed.* Without tenacity, talent and preparation mean little. With it, you become unstoppable.

When I first began coaching football, I always used this expression with my athletes: "Someone out there is training right now to beat you." Much like internal discipline, tenacity is one of the grittier habits we can cultivate. That's why I love placing it at the end of *The CRUSH-IT Formula*—discipline and tenacity are what separate the good from the great. They are the difference between silver and gold, between almost making it and standing at the top of the podium.

So, how do we build tenacity? I get this question from clients all the time. *How can I be more tenacious? How do I develop persistence?* The simple answer is by intentionally pushing your limits, embracing discomfort, and refusing to quit when things get tough. Tenacity isn't something you're born with—it's something you train.

PERSISTENCE

Researchers conducted a study, "Evidence for a Behaviourally Measurable Perseverance Trait in Humans,"[1] to measure perseverance in humans, testing both physical and mental persistence. Participants completed six challenging tasks, including endurance exercises, problem-solving exercises, and monotonous activities, and their ability to persist through discomfort and difficulty was recorded to determine patterns in perseverance.

The results showed that perseverance can be divided into two key types: physical (like enduring pain or physical strain) and mental (like solving tough problems or staying engaged in boring tasks). Interestingly, some tasks engaged both aspects, while others, like an anagram challenge, did not fit neatly into either category.

One of the study's most important findings challenges the idea of ego depletion (which we discussed in the chapter on discipline), the belief that using self-control drains mental energy. Instead, researchers found that people who persisted in one task were likely to persist in others, suggesting that perseverance is a stable personality trait rather than something that simply wears out. They also examined biological factors like heart rate, age, and stress levels but found little connection between these and perseverance. However, lower heart rates during difficult tasks were linked to higher endurance, possibly indicating that stress resilience plays a role in persistence.

This study highlights that perseverance is a measurable and trainable trait, not just a momentary act of willpower. It suggests that building

---

1. Määttänen, Ilmari, Emilia Makkonen, Markus Jokela, Johanna Närväinen, Julius Väliaho, Vilja Seppälä, Julia Kylmälä, and Pentti Henttonen. "Evidence for a Behaviourally Measurable Perseverance Trait in Humans." *Behavioral Sciences* 11, no. 9 (September 9, 2021): 123. https://doi.org/10.3390/bs11090123.

persistence in one area of life can strengthen it in others, and that pushing through discomfort is more about mindset than biology. Understanding this can help individuals and organizations develop strategies to build resilience and improve. So how do you build persistence? Be more determined. How do you develop resilience? Be more resilient. How do I improve focus? Just focus.

These are the short, simple answers, but that's not why you're here. You're working through this model because you know true perseverance requires more than vague advice. There are specific habits and strategies you can develop to increase your persistence, strengthen your determination, and sharpen your focus so you can stay locked onto a goal for the long haul without getting easily distracted. The ability to sustain prolonged physical or mental effort endurance is something you can tap into. But it requires patience, and patience is one of the most critical aspects of tenacity. Pushing through challenges without getting discouraged is hard, but it comes down to a simple question: what do you want your life to be about?

Will you choose a life of potential and avoidance, backing down when things get tough? Or will you choose a life where you elevate, rise above challenges, and prove to yourself what you're truly capable of? In the last chapter, we discussed the two percent mindset—those who refuse to settle. Now, we'll dive into how you can join that elite group and elevate yourself to the next level.

PATIENCE AND PERSEVERANCE: THE HOURS THAT SHAPE YOU

When we think about tenacity, the image that often comes to mind is a bulldog—small but fierce and packed with determination, drive, and relentless spirit. That's what tenacity looks like in action. But what we can't always define is how long it takes to achieve our goals. We measure progress, put in the effort, and expect results. Some people invest five hours into something and wonder why they haven't improved. Others put in 100 hours and still see no change. Sometimes it takes 500 hours. Sometimes it takes 5,000. Growth isn't linear, and it often feels like nothing is happening.

Dr. Nate Zinsser in *The Confident Mind* talks about this in relation to confidence, how we experience rapid improvement at first, followed by long plateaus where progress feels stagnant. This is where most people quit, assuming they've hit their limit. But in reality, growth is happening beneath the surface. Confidence and perseverance are built in these moments of doubt, and this is where tenacity matters most. It's a test of patience—years of practicing the fundamentals, yet no championship trophy, late nights at the office, yet no promotion, eating right, yet little weight lost.

We've all been there. The effort is there, but the results feel slow. And before we see the breakthroughs, we need patience. Perseverance isn't just about effort—it's about enduring the wait. True success requires staying the course, even when it feels like nothing is happening. Because, in the end, persistence plus patience equals progress. We develop endurance as we stay patient through the process.

The real question isn't whether or not you can do it but *what you need to believe* to get there. Our beliefs shape our potential. Without a clear vision of success, it's hard to stay committed. Clarity is a high-performance habit, and without it, self-doubt takes over. Your beliefs define your capacity. They determine how well you can tap into your strengths, talents, and resources—how you tap into all of you. The way you see yourself affects everything: your focus, resilience, and determination. So ask yourself:

- What do I need to believe about myself to keep going?
- Do I see myself as someone who persists, endures, thrives under pressure, sees the vision?

CONFIDENCE

A huge component of tenacity comes from having an unshakable belief in yourself. The world's highest achievers persist because they have an underlying confidence that keeps them going, no matter the obstacles. If you ask someone to define confidence, most will say it's simply believing in yourself or knowing you can do something. But I have learned that true confidence comes when we can eliminate thinking and execute automatically. This means that true confidence isn't just belief, it's the ability to act instinctively, especially in the face of setbacks.

There were moments in my career where I felt this level of clarity and instinctive execution—one of them was the night of the 2016 Grey Cup. That night, I knew exactly where I was going with every play call. If you remember from the previous chapter, I explained how play callers sometimes get "stuck" during a game, hesitating, second-guessing, or scrambling for the right decision. But that night, I wasn't stuck. I knew what to do in every scenario, including a crucial second play of the game where we faced second down and 21 (for context, Canadian football has only three downs, making it faster-paced and more pass-oriented). We had missed a golden opportunity on the first play of the game, but it didn't shake me. I didn't dwell on it or hesitate. I already knew the exact call for that situation, and I executed without hesitation. And I did that the entire night.

Being persistent and tenacious means you don't hesitate or overthink failure—you push forward automatically. This doesn't mean you don't feel disappointment, frustration, or exhaustion. But when you're truly CRUSHING-IT, you've mastered the art of failing, learning, and rising again. It becomes second nature. Developing this confidence in your ability to persevere starts with a clear purpose.

DEVELOP A CLEAR PURPOSE

Pushing through to your goals is nearly impossible if you lack clarity on your why. Without a clear purpose, endurance becomes a struggle, and persistence fades when challenges arise. Chasing a goal is one thing, but having a deep understanding of your purpose is what separates those who keep going from those who eventually burn out.

When it comes to tenacity, I see people fall into two categories. The first group consists of those who have spent their whole lives grinding. They are resilient, disciplined, and relentless in their pursuit of success. They have an incredible ability to push through hardship, but they lack clarity on why they are pushing themselves so hard. They wake up every day and give their best, yet they haven't truly defined their purpose or vision. The second group has the same drive, the same grit, and the same relentless work ethic, but there's one key difference—they have extreme clarity around their purpose. They know exactly why they are sacrificing, why they are training, why they demand so much from themselves. Their vision and purpose are fully aligned, giving them an internal fire that fuels them through every challenge.

The first group will still accomplish great things. They will outperform the average and push further than most. But at some point, when life throws its hardest obstacles their way, they will start to question everything. They will ask themselves, *Why am I doing this? What is it all for?* For many, that's where the road ends. The second group, the ones who are deeply connected to their purpose, will go much farther when things get tough. When life knocks them down, their *why* keeps them standing back up. They don't just survive setbacks—they thrive in them. Because when you have clarity of purpose, obstacles don't stop you. They fuel you.

EVERYTHING IS FEEDBACK: HOW YOU PROCESS IT MATTERS

Every opportunity is feedback—every success, failure, misstep, victory, and even near-miss provides valuable information. Feedback shows us where we excel, where we need to adjust, and how to fine-tune our approach. But simply acknowledging feedback isn't enough. Two key factors determine whether it helps or hinders your progress:

1. **The lens through which you see it.** The way you interpret feedback matters. If you see setbacks as personal failures, they can drain your confidence and make you hesitant. But if you view them as data points and stepping stones toward mastery, they become valuable tools for improvement.
2. **What you do with it.** Feedback alone changes nothing; how you respond is what determines growth. Do you adapt, adjust, and move forward, or do you dwell on mistakes and let them define you?

When we adopt the former mindset, setbacks stop being roadblocks and instead become part of the process. This shift prevents us from self-judgment and frustration for not being where we want to be. Instead of dwelling on what went wrong, we analyze, adjust, and move forward with greater clarity.

By treating every moment as feedback, we reinforce the habits that matter: discipline, resilience, and focus. These habits build endurance and the ability to persevere. Instead of letting setbacks define us, we lean into our training, preparation, and routines that support success. We stop obsessing over the outcome and instead commit to showing up with intention and purpose, refining our approach, and attacking the next challenge with even greater precision. But to truly apply this perspective, you must develop the ability to stay neutral.

I struggled with this for a long time. I took losses unhealthily hard. If we lost, I would dissect the game until I found something that made it my fault, be it a play call, a missed adjustment, or something I failed to teach properly. And instead of using that feedback constructively, I used it to beat myself up. Yes, I would bounce back, but only after internalizing the feedback with a heavy dose of negative emotion. I knew I couldn't last as a coordinator if I didn't change this.

One day, I had a simple but powerful realization. It's just feedback. How I chose to interpret it was 100 percent on me. This shift changed everything. Every decision—right or wrong—gave me immediate feedback, and once I saw it that way, I stopped allowing self-criticism to get in the way and started making faster, better adjustments. I even carried this mindset into my own company:

- Lose a potential client? Feedback. Adjust. Move on.
- Feeling overwhelmed by too many clients? Feedback. Adapt. Create better systems.

This shift eliminated the emotional drain of failure and regret and replaced it with a process-driven approach. Because when you see everything as feedback, you grow.

TAKE CONTINUOUS ACTION

Tenacity is about taking action—repeatedly—even when progress is slow and obstacles surface. The more action you take, the stronger your persistence becomes. Action creates momentum, and the hardest part of facing challenges is getting started or getting started again after a setback. Once you take action, even baby steps, momentum begins to build, and with each step forward, you are reinforcing your ability to persist and training your mind to push through resistance.

Actions also reduce fear and hesitation. When you hesitate, overanalyze, or let doubt creep in, you delay. Doubt creates delay. Delay creates a divide inside of you. Taking action minimizes hesitation because it shifts your focus from "what if" to "what's next." Being comfortable with discomfort is a key aspect of tenacity. Consistently taking action, which requires discipline, reinforces self-efficacy and builds on your problem-solving skills. The ability to adapt and adjust is the result of taking action, and when you take continuous action, you are bound to hit obstacles, and you put yourself in a situation where you have to figure things out.

Taking action shifts your sense of who you are. Your identity transforms, and you start to see yourself as someone who just doesn't give up. Taking action programs your subconscious, and you find yourself instinctively pushing yourself forward because it's just who you are.

THE DRIVE TO ACHIEVE: BUILT, NOT BORN

After my football career ended, I remember desperately wanting to be part of a team again. I missed the camaraderie, the shared purpose, and the feeling of working toward something bigger than myself. That's why, as I shared earlier, I picked up a tennis racket. What I didn't share, however, is that despite going on to play at the collegiate level and even competing in small professional tournaments, I didn't make the team at first. In fact, I didn't make it the second time either. I still remember my high school coach telling me, "You can practice with us, but unfortunately, there's no room for you on the team."

So, in 110-degree heat, I showed up anyway. I was the first one out there and the last one to leave by hours. Since I wasn't officially on the team, I couldn't participate in all the drills, so I took a bucket of balls and practiced serving—over and over again. With so much repetition, I became exceptional at serving, but that was just one piece of the game. Most people would have gotten bored. I didn't. I kept showing up, day after day, long after everyone else had gone home. I wasn't sure what drove me at 13 years old but looking back, I know exactly what it was. Tenacity.

This relentless drive wasn't always in me. I wasn't born with it. I didn't grow up in a high-achieving environment, nor was I naturally wired for success. But looking back, it's clear it was there all along, shaping my path. It's what pushed me to pursue a law degree when the odds were against me. It's what kept me going when I was told I'd never be more than a high school coach. It's what helped me pivot when the world was thrown into chaos during the pandemic. It's what led me to win a championship and become one of only forty-one head coaches in the world to have done that. And it's what drives me today: the relentless pursuit of achievement, not just for myself, but to leave a mark, impact others, and help them find their own greatness.

This drive isn't just about personal success—it fuels me to help others avoid the missteps I made. To show them that by doing the hard work, shifting their mindset, and redefining how they see themselves, they too can build a life of excellence.

THE 28 PERCENT RULE: WINNING THE TIME OTHERS WASTE

One of the greatest benefits of coaching teams and communities is the ability to learn from others. I'll be honest. The 28 Percent Rule isn't something I created. It was shared with me, and once I understood it, I realized it was one of the most powerful concepts for developing discipline and maximizing time. So, what is the 28 Percent Rule? It's simple: 28 percent of our week is made up of weekends. That's more than a quarter of our time. And for as long as I can remember, I've followed this rule without even knowing it. I used to text my players—now I text my clients and teams—asking the question: *"How are you winning this weekend?"*

Most people take the weekend off. They sleep in, relax by the pool, or unwind at the beach. And while rest is important, consistently losing 28 percent of your time to leisure adds up fast. Imagine losing over a quarter of your opportunity to grow, improve, and achieve your goals simply by taking weekends off. Now, I'm not saying you shouldn't recharge—you absolutely should. But if you take every weekend off, you better be operating at an unmatched and unparalleled level during the other five days. And the reality is that most people aren't. That's why the 28 Percent Rule is so powerful. It's about taking advantage of the time that most people waste.

But it's not just about working more—it's about working smarter. I challenge my clients not just to grind through weekends but to use that time to become the highest version of themselves. What skills do you need to develop? How can you dedicate this time to improving your business, training, or personal performance? What areas of growth have been neglected during the week that you can focus on?

The 28 Percent Rule is an unbelievable way to maximize time. It requires persistence, intention, and the willingness to keep pushing forward despite obstacles or setbacks. And in the long run, it's a game-changer for those who are willing to use their time differently.

Back to my daughter. I knew she was determined, but I was hot and thirsty, so I asked, "Sweetheart, do you really want to do this?" She gave me *the look*—you know, the one that says, *That's a dumb question, and I'm not dignifying it with an answer.* So I said, "Then I need you to do this: close your eyes and keep them closed. See yourself doing it first. You have to visualize it before you make it happen." She stood there, eyes shut, for about 20 seconds. Then, without hesitation, she opened her eyes, jumped up, grabbed the pull-up bar, and pulled herself up like she had been doing it for years. I was blown away. I knew I was a good mindset and performance coach, but this was next-level. It was a powerful reminder of what visualization can do and the unstoppable force of sheer tenacity. Most of all, I was blown away by my daughter.

CHAPTER 8
CRUSH-IT AS A LEADER

As we transition into the second part of this book, we dive into *The CRUSH-IT Formula* as it applies to leadership—a crucial phase where the framework shifts from personal growth to guiding others effectively. In the first section, we explored how *The CRUSH-IT Formula* helps you build resilience, establish strong habits, and tap into your internal strengths. But once you've cultivated these qualities, how do you use them to lead?

Ever wonder how our brains seem wired to receive sudden bursts of insight, or what I call "downloads" from the universe? The CRUSH-IT model began to take shape through one of these moments, with one key thought repeating itself in the background: *The framework needs to have a broad impact. It has to be applicable across different areas of life and work.* As I refined, I kept asking myself:

- What does CRUSH-IT look like in different areas for different people?
- How can this acronym serve as a practical tool to empower us?
- How can it help measure effectiveness across multiple domains?

With these questions in mind, the CRUSH-IT model became more than just an idea—it became a guide for maximizing performance and potential. As I shifted my focus to leadership, I realized that the same principles could be applied with slight adjustments to suit the unique demands of guiding and influencing others. The first question that came to mind was, what does it mean to CRUSH-IT as a leader? So, I decided to take the same acronym and adjust it slightly to create a powerful framework for leadership. Here's how it looks:

C = Connection
R = Reliability
U = Unity
S = Service
H = Honesty
I = Intentionality
T = Trust

In the following pages, we'll explore how these qualities help you not only step into leadership but also lead with purpose, impact, and effectiveness, no matter the scale.

THE POWER OF CONNECTION

If you want to crush it as a leader, the first thing you must hone in on is **connection**—and I don't mean surface-level connection, where you casually say hello in the hallway and ask about someone's weekend. I mean deep, meaningful connection.

Research shows that the best leaders create meaningful connections in three key ways: first, they show up with vulnerability; second, they demonstrate genuine interest in others; and finally, they lift others up.

VULNERABILITY

This isn't a book designed to teach you what to say or how to say it. But if you want to be a leader that truly connects, you have to be willing to share. You must be open enough to communicate in a way that enables people to resonate with you, and to do so, you must let them see who you really are, the mistakes you've made, and the fact that you are human, just like them. This requires vulnerability.

The point of vulnerability is to show the authentic side of who you are, the part you might normally keep private. I have found that there are two ways I do this.

The first is by being honest about your struggles and your mistakes. Start small, and when you're struggling with a task, be honest and ask for help. When you are struggling with your teenage daughter, share the struggle. In these small moments, you create connection and show up authentically by saying it's okay to be honest about difficult things. You must also be genuinely interested in the lives of the people you lead. We covered this in Chapter 4. The second way to create deep connection through vulnerability is by doing the difficult thing, even when others hesitate. Leadership is about influence, and influence is built when someone steps up to do what's right, even when it's uncomfortable. Let me give you an example.

A few days after 9/11, I was in my second year of law school at American University in Washington, D.C. At the time, I was also working at a firm on the Potomac River, where the rooftop offered some of the best views of the city. We all remember the tragedy of that day, and the days that followed were filled with shock, grief, and uncertainty. When we returned to class on September 13th, I witnessed two completely different approaches to leadership. One professor didn't acknowledge what had happened at all—he simply launched into his lecture, as if nothing had changed. Now, I'm not judging him; perhaps that was his way of coping.

But another professor took a different approach. She started class by simply asking, "How is everyone feeling?" That simple question led to an hour and a half of raw, emotional conversation—we talked, we cried, and we let our anger surface. It was a difficult conversation, especially in an international law school with diverse perspectives, but it was exactly what everyone needed. That moment created a deeper connection. She didn't avoid the discomfort—she leaned into it. That's what true leaders do. They step forward when it's hard, when it's uncertain, and when it matters most.

GENUINE INTEREST

After one of our games, I was in the locker room, picking up trash off the floor. At the time, I was the offensive coordinator for the Ottawa Redblacks, and as I walked through, the equipment manager came by, a guy whose job, along with his staff, was to clean up the locker room after every game. In football, equipment managers are the unsung heroes. They handle everything behind the scenes to ensure the team can function on game day—setting up the field, fixing gear malfunctions, making sure every player has the right socks. They're the glue that holds everything together, yet they rarely get the recognition they deserve.

The beauty of equipment managers is that they are always in the locker room. They see everything. They connect with players in ways coaches sometimes can't because they're there for the little moments, building relationships without pretense or expectation. As I picked up trash, the equipment manager looked at me and said, "Coach, you don't have to do that. I got this." We had just lost a tough game, and instead of leaving, I sat down with him. We both picked up trash and started talking. That moment reinforced something for me. Leadership is about connection. It's about taking the time to engage with people, to understand them beyond their roles. As I discussed in Chapter 3, this was Drew Brees' greatest gift—the ability to connect with people on an emotional level.

In professional football, we operate in pods, offense, defense, and special teams. As an offensive coordinator, my job was to design the offensive game plan, coordinate with the entire offensive staff, and ensure every position coach and assistant was aligned with our strategy. In pro football, each position has its own coach, sometimes two, with additional assistants supporting them. The list of personnel can be extensive, making coordination crucial. The year after winning the Grey Cup, we went right back to work, but it wasn't the same. We had lost key players, our quarterback retired, contracts weren't renewed for two of our receivers, and we saw several departures on defense due to retirements and roster changes.

Heading into the new season, there was excitement about the fresh talent we had brought in, but there was also a lot of uncertainty. And I made a mistake—I spent the first seven games solely focused on game planning, on the X's and O's, without truly connecting with my players and coaches. That mistake cost us. We started the season 1–6, struggling to find our rhythm. Although we fought our way back into the playoffs, the turning point wasn't in the strategy; it was in the people. The moment I shifted my focus from the plan to the players, everything changed.

I remember walking out of the locker room late one night with a deeper understanding of what connection truly means. Beyond vulnerability, true leadership is about a genuine interest in people—what drives them, what they need to succeed, and what they need when struggling.

LIFTING OTHERS UP

Beyond demonstrating vulnerability and genuine interest in others, the final component of true connection is elevation, or the mindset of lifting others up.

Ask yourself:

- How can this person feel more inspired after our conversation?
- How can I elevate them, empower them, and help them grow?

In 2018, we overhauled our coaching staff and roster in a big way. But this time, I wasn't going to make the same mistake twice. I knew that before we could win on the field, we had to connect as a team. I introduced the fisherman story. I stood in front of the offensive team room and asked, "What happens when two guys go fishing?"

A voice from the back of the room called out, "They drink a lot of beer."

I chuckled. "That might be true, but what else happens?"

A different player spoke up, a kid from deep in the south, his accent thick and unmistakable. He said, "They talk."

I loved that answer. To reinforce the importance of sharing and connection, I placed a fisherman's stool in the front of the meeting room. Every so often, I'd bring a player up and have him share his story so we could truly get to know him not just as an athlete, but as a person.

One day, I called up a six-foot, four-inch, 225-pound receiver—a guy who looked exactly how I think I look (Ha!).

I asked him, "What are you most grateful for?"

He smiled and gave a typical answer: "Oh, Coach, I'm thankful for my teammates, the coaches, and you."

I nodded. "That's great. But what else are you grateful for?"

His smile faded slightly. He hesitated, then said, "Coach, where I grew up, sometimes football practice would get canceled because there were gunshots in the neighborhood. We might have only practiced two or three times a week." The room got quiet. He continued, "Football's always been hard for me. But you know what I'm most grateful for?"

I leaned in. "What?"

"My bed."

The silence in the room became deafening. I asked him, "You mean, you finally have your own bedroom?"

He shook his head. "No, Coach. I have my own bed for the first time in my life."

Twenty-four years. He had spent his entire life sleeping on the floor or a couch. In that moment, the team changed. Every player in that room silently committed to doing everything in their power to help this young man experience the joy of winning.

That moment wasn't about football—it was about elevation. It was about lifting someone up that needed it. That's what great leaders do.

RELIABILITY: THE SILENT SUPERPOWER OF GREAT LEADERS

Are you reliable? Whenever I pose this question on stage, hands shoot up across the room. Most people believe they are. And when I ask the question, "How do you measure your reliability?" the answers vary. "People can count on me." "I show up." "I do what I say I'm going to do." That's a good start, but true reliability goes deeper.

To start, reliability and integrity are often tied together. The real

THE CRUSH-IT FORMULA

question isn't just whether you do what you say you'll do, but how often you'll do it. Nobody is perfect. Life happens. Things come up. But if you were graded on reliability, what would your score be? Would you be 70 percent reliable? 80 percent? Would your rating be different at work than at home? Great leaders understand that reliability is one of the most valuable traits they can develop, and it starts with consistent messaging.

Years ago, I fell into the trap of constantly changing the focus of my messaging. Each week, I had a new theme or a different area of emphasis. But instead of making me more reliable, it created confusion.

Consistency in messaging eliminates uncertainty. It builds trust. When people hear the same clear and steady message, they know what to expect, and that creates a sense of reliability.

Another aspect of reliability is ownership. The best leaders take full responsibility for their actions—no excuses, no blame. The Navy SEALs have a saying: "Extreme Ownership." In his book by the same name, Jocko Willink explains that everything that happens on a mission is the leader's responsibility—no exceptions. The same principle applies to leadership in any field. We've all heard the phrase: "Be a thumb pointer, not a finger pointer." Great leaders own their mistakes and give credit to others when things go well.

After a tough game, I would walk into the meeting room and tell the team, "That was a bad call. That's on me." I'd literally pound my chest with my thumb—owning the mistake in front of everyone. The first few times, the room was silent. No reaction. But I kept doing it, not as a tactic, but because it was the truth. I could have made a better call. I should have done better. By owning it, I wasn't just holding myself accountable; I was creating a culture of ownership in that room.

Over time, things started to change. The quarterback would say, "No, Coach, that was a great call. I need to locate the ball a little bit better. I need to throw a better pass." Then, you would hear the receivers chime up from the other side of the room. "Nope, that is B.S. That ball was on my fingertips. I need to catch that. That is not on you, Trevor." Then somebody from the back of the room where the big hogs sit would say, "That is not on either of you. Trevor, how could you even throw that ball? You had a hand right in your face. That one is on me. I have got to block that defender better." Creating this level of ownership only comes when you start pointing your thumb at yourself.

True reliability creates an unshakable sense of trust, the belief that the person leading us is someone we can count on—that no matter what happens, they have our back. Ultimately, reliability is measured in the trenches. When things go wrong, do people know you'll stand beside them and take accountability? That's what separates true leaders from those who just hold a title. This doesn't mean leadership is without hard decisions, especially in pro football. Players get cut, released, traded, promoted, or demoted every week. One moment, you're starting, the next, you're sidelined, and your income depends on it. I share this because many people believe extreme ownership isn't possible in business. I often hear, "I can't do that. People will take advantage of me." But in sports where careers are on the line every day, the best leaders still operate with this level of accountability. And the more reliable you are, the stronger your ability to hold others accountable. Extreme ownership, consistency, dependability, and accountability all work together. When you master them, you don't just become a better leader—you become the leader people trust, no matter the circumstances.

"WHAT DOES THE "U" STAND FOR?"

I can't tell you how many times I've been asked this question. When people dive into the CRUSH-IT framework, they get excited, anticipating what each letter stands for. I've had people ask me over and over, "What does the U stand for?"

In the context of leadership, it stands for unity. Now, you might ask, "Wait...isn't unification the same as connection?" Not even close. Connection and unity are different. Many great leaders know how to connect with people, but it takes special skill to bring entire groups together, create alignment, and turn individuals into a cohesive force.

I don't claim to be an expert, but I love studying behavior. And after spending most of my career working with 20- to 28-year-olds, I've developed a keen sense for it. Football is full of big personalities, ambition, and plenty of B.S. I was the same way at that age. These young men are competing for their dreams, so naturally, walls go up. But when trust is built, connection is established, and reliability is proven, barriers start to break down.

That's when you see true unification: when a player or teammate wants success more for the person next to them than they do for themselves. That's the defining quality of championship teams and elite cultures.

That's not always the case, especially in large companies and organizations, but the best teams share one common trait: they work for the person next to them. Take that talented receiver we talked about, the one who, at 24 years old, finally had his own bed. What really happened in that locker room was bigger than football. Every single person in that room, most of whom had already won one or two Grey Cups, wanted that young man to experience the joy of winning one for himself. When a team reaches that level, where they want success for someone else more than they want it for themselves, that's the mark of a leader who has truly unified a group.

And let's be honest. This is one of the hardest things to do, especially as the size of the team, company, or egos increases. But as a leader, dealing with egos isn't optional; it's part of the job. How well you navigate them determines whether you're just managing people or truly bringing them together.

Everyone unifies differently. There's no one-size-fits-all approach to bringing people together. But if you're crushing it as a leader, you have a clear and intentional plan for how to do it. And it goes far beyond a company barbecue or Friday night happy hours. Those things matter, but they're not enough. True unification requires thoughtful, ongoing effort. That's why I love asking leaders around the world how they bring their teams together and what unique things they do to foster connection and alignment. The answer often depends on the company's culture, but the key takeaway is simple: if you're truly leading at a high level, you're not just managing people. You're uniting them.

I will give you four quick suggestions:

Number one is to break bread together. Gregg Popovich, the legendary San Antonio Spurs coach, is well known for emphasizing the importance of team bonding, camaraderie, and shared meals as a crucial part of building a strong team culture. Popovich has often spoken about the value of breaking bread together—literally sitting down for meals as a team—to develop trust and chemistry. He believes that spending time together off the court fosters deeper relationships, which then translate to better teamwork on the court.

Here are some key points about Popovich's philosophy on team meals:

- **Building relationships.** He sees meals as a way to truly get to know each other beyond basketball.
- **Cultural exchange.** He often introduces players to different cuisines to expand their perspectives.
- **Creating open communication**. By removing distractions and sitting together, he fosters meaningful conversations among players and coaches.
- **Establishing a family atmosphere.** He treats his players like family, and meals are a way to reinforce that bond.

He has famously taken Spurs teams (and even Team USA) to top-tier restaurants worldwide, using food as a medium to connect his players. He took this concept further in recruiting Tim Duncan, affectionately known as the "Big Fundamental" to the Spurs. Popovich talks about how he spent three days in the Virgin Islands, where Duncan lived, and they spent that time hanging out on the beach, talking about life, family, and philosophy rather than just basketball. They did not talk about basketball once during those three days. If you want to unify your team, follow Poppovich's example.

Number two is to involve staff or team members in your decisions. Giving them a sense of ownership builds trust and says, "I value you and your thoughts." That is more important to many than finances or recognition. This can also be done when setting your fundamentals. Get feedback, bring in Uber Eats, and develop a sense of "let's figure things out together."

Number three is to trust your team to make adjustments and suggestions. There were several moments in my coaching career when players approached me mid-game, suggesting an adjustment to a play we had run weeks earlier based on how the defense was reacting. As a coach, you try to control every scenario, but I was open to their insight. We made the change, called the play, and scored a touchdown. But here's the key. If it had failed, I would have taken full accountability. If it succeeded, I gave them all the credit. Nothing unifies a team more than knowing their leader has their back. When people feel trusted and valued, they don't just execute plays—they own them.

Number four is to make room for dissent. A strong organizational culture allows for disagreement and creates space for it. This means acknowledging that there won't always be full agreement on an issue or topic but practicing courageous conversation anyway. Ensure everyone "has an at bat" (gets their turn to be heard). I love how this concept is applied at Airbnb, where one of their values, "allowing for disagreement," was put into action as a behavior and titled **"Elephants, Dead Fish, and Vomit."** It meant they were always going to address the elephants in the room, they were going to talk about the stinky stuff (dead fish), and they were going to get their feelings out (vomit). As a result of this principle, Airbnb created an environment where disagreement and different opinions were welcomed.

SERVICE: ENABLING VERSUS EMPOWERING

The best leaders serve the needs of others, but there's a big difference between enabling and serving. Serving others means helping them succeed, developing their skills, challenging them to grow, and guiding them toward becoming their best selves. It's not just about offering support; sometimes, it requires pointing out blind spots, addressing inconsistencies, and holding people accountable. True leadership is about investing in your people, not simply doing things for them.

There's a subtle but powerful distinction between the questions:

- "How can I help you?" (which can invite dependency)
- "What do you need from me?" (which fosters growth and responsibility)

I learned this lesson the hard way early in my career as an offensive coordinator. I would ask my staff, "How can I help you?" and suddenly, I found myself taking on extra work, covering for others, or handling tasks they should have been doing themselves. That wasn't leadership, and it enabled responses like:

- *"Can you do this for me?"*
- *"I'm not sure how to do this."*
- *"It's going to take me longer to do than it would take you."*

Each time, I thought I was helping, but all I did was create frustration for them and for myself. I was removing their responsibility instead of empowering them to take ownership.

Real service-based leadership isn't about doing the work for others —it's about teaching, mentoring, and developing people so they can thrive on their own. It's about challenging them to rise, not rescuing them from difficulty. When leaders serve with the right mindset, they don't just build stronger teams they build future leaders.

Servant leadership is about helping people step into their future selves today, but that process doesn't mean taking over for them. It means guiding, supporting, and empowering them to take ownership of their growth. One simple yet powerful shift in this approach starts with asking the right questions. Instead of asking, "How can I help you?" I encourage leaders to ask, "What do you need from me?" This question still offers support, but it places responsibility back on the individual, challenging them to identify their needs and take an active role in their own development.

When working with clients, I ask them:

- "What percentage of your time is spent serving others?"
- "What do you think that percentage should be?"

The answers are revealing. Regardless of what level you lead at, serving others is always part of the job, but it should have balance.

When I think back on the best leaders I've had the privilege to work with, one name stands out: Pete Mangurian. During my early years as an offensive coordinator at Columbia University, we were struggling. I mean really struggling. Despite that, Pete trusted me to take the reins of the offense and install a system modeled after the New England Patriots' approach.

One day, he gave me an assignment that changed the way I coach and lead. "I want you to film yourself installing the entire system," he said, "then go back and watch it." Pete could have easily told me what I was doing wrong, but instead, he challenged me to see it for myself and improve. So, I did. And when I watched myself teaching on film, I saw immediately the gaps, the jumps, the missing pieces, even the moments when I pivoted to unrelated information instead of staying focused.

It was a powerful realization. When we teach, we have to communicate at the level required for maximum understanding. That lesson stuck with me. Pete didn't just critique me; he empowered me to refine, improve, and take ownership of my own development. And that's what great leaders do. Even as I write this, I am still working on repeating it and saying it better. It is making me a better presenter, speaker, and leader.

Great leaders understand what individuals need for growth, even when those individuals don't always recognize it themselves. They tap into strengths, challenge people to push further, and create intentional opportunities for development. The true mark of a leader isn't just what they achieve; it's how many people elevate themselves. A leader's legacy is measured by the number of individuals they help reach their full potential and the lasting impact they leave behind. As the saying goes, "The secret of institution-building is to weld a team together by lifting them up to grow taller than they would otherwise be."

Servant leaders embody this philosophy. They are deeply committed to the growth of their team, not just as employees but as people. They recognize the intrinsic value of their team members and the value that extends beyond their day-to-day contributions or the financial success they bring to the organization. True servant leadership is about nurturing both personal and professional growth. This happens through learning opportunities, training, development, and bringing in outside coaches and continuous support. It's reinforced through mentorship, coaching, honest feedback, and an environment that encourages autonomy and accountability. By lifting others up, empowering them to take ownership, and fostering a culture of trust and development, servant leaders don't just create short-term success they build a lasting legacy of growth, rooted in honesty.

HONESTY

This section isn't about honesty in the basic sense of being truthful but a deeper level of honesty, the kind that requires you to be brutally honest with yourself. This means taking a hard look in the mirror and assessing:

- How am I truly showing up?
- Am I consistent, or do I fall short in key areas?
- Is my messaging consistent?
- Am I leading with reliability, or do I waver under pressure?
- How do I handle my team when I feel stressed?
- Am I embodying the principles and values I want to see in them? Am I doing this all the time?

If you're going to crush it as a leader, honesty isn't optional, it's essential. It's the internal compass that allows you to self-correct before anyone else has to. And that's hard for most people. I'd argue that only the top two to three percent of the best leaders in the world have truly mastered this skill—the ability to step back, reflect, and pinpoint where they are lacking because honesty and ownership are directly linked. Without one, the other can't exist. I had to face this reality when I let go of a coach and a friend that I had hired. When I looked back at it, I had to confront the reality that my decision-making process, and the way I had put him in a difficult situation, had set him up for an uphill battle. That realization forced me to take a deep, honest look at myself. I had to admit that I had failed him—in more ways than one. It was a hard lesson and one that still stings today. It might have felt right at the time, but the reflection showed me it was a leadership failure on my part.

One of the hardest parts of being a leader, whether you're a CEO, head coach, or company leader, is the constant self-reflection. *Did that message land the way I intended? Did I communicate that effectively? Could I have handled that situation better?* Leadership can be isolating. It's hard and lonely at the top, but regularly assessing yourself, your actions, your decisions, and your impact is what gives you longevity as a leader. These moments of honesty are hallmarks of great leadership. But self-awareness alone isn't enough. There's a second layer to honesty that many leaders struggle with: being honest about your team's performance. Too often, we see leaders deflect accountability, saying things like, "We're doing the best we can under the circumstances." And while there may be truth in that, great leaders don't settle for excuses. They address reality head-on.

Being honest with your team—about their shortcomings and their performance, and with each individual—requires having difficult conversations. It means acknowledging where they stand, evaluating their contributions, and sometimes making tough decisions about people you deeply care about. There are moments when, despite how much you value someone, you must accept that they no longer belong on the team.

A true leader embraces this responsibility, honestly assessing necessary changes, even when those decisions are difficult. Leadership isn't just about investing in people—it's about investing in them through honesty. That means clearly communicating the level of performance required and where they stand in relation to it, whether they are meeting expectations or falling short. Honest leadership isn't always easy, but it's always necessary.

We had to have these hard conversations in football every week. A player was on the active roster one week, receiving a full game check, and then the next week, he was downgraded to the practice squad, where his check for the week may not have been even five percent of a game check. For those of you who don't know, in football and other sports, players are paid their entire salary over the course of a season.

So if there are 17 games, they receive their contract, excluding bonuses, split equally over those 17 weeks. You can imagine what being relegated to the practice squad for that week means financially. In these conversations, you had to be brutally honest, even at times when it had nothing to do with their performance and everything to do with things outside of their control, like injuries to other positions, which affected the overall roster makeup. I've seen others try to tell other players that their performance or lack thereof was the reason they were relegated to the practice squad that week, and it would always backfire—talk about losing trust. In these moments, the direct and honest approach matters. Sometimes being honest sucks, but it's the right thing to do.

INTENTIONALITY

Intentionality in leadership means being deliberate and purposeful in your actions and decisions. It's about having a clear plan and executing it with precision. When you're truly excelling as a leader, your intentionality shines through. Think of a football practice, which is something we touched on earlier. There's so much movement, crispness, and sharpness; it's like a well-coordinated military exercise. The horn blows, the whistles sound, and everyone transitions seamlessly from one drill to the next. No time is wasted. On the best teams, the ball is spotted, and within 10 seconds, the next drill has started. "Where are the scripts? Where is the practice plan?" These are questions I've heard throughout my entire career.

When you attend a football practice, every minute is scripted down to the finest detail—it's incredible to witness. Whenever possible, I take some of my top clients to practices at elite college or professional teams so they can see this level of intentional execution firsthand.

In football, we follow a practice plan down to the second. It outlines what each coach is working on, which scenarios are being practiced, where on the field each drill takes place, and what equipment is needed.

A typical practice consists of 12 to 18 periods, each signaled by a horn to mark the transition. When the horn blows, it's orchestrated chaos, with players and coaches moving seamlessly to their next station, getting set, and starting the next drill within seconds. The best teams move like a symphony, transitioning just before the horn sounds so they're in position and ready the moment the next period begins. It's precision at its finest. Beyond the practice plan, each period also has an offensive or defensive script, a structured sequence of plays designed to focus on specific situations, down-and-distance scenarios, and game plans. Every detail is choreographed to ensure maximum efficiency and preparedness.

On the practice field, we hold ourselves accountable through a structured process that ensures discipline, attention to detail, and continuous improvement. Every action, whether it's an incorrect substitution, a player showing up late, or jumping offside, has both a consequence and a learning moment attached to it.

Everything we do has a process. Processes remove doubt and uncertainty, which, in turn, eliminates anxiety. That's why we have a structured approach to everything. After watching a practice with my clients, I turn to them and ask:

- What is your process for running meetings?
- What is your process for handling change?
- What is your process for accountability?

Operating with this level of intentionality is what separates the next echelon of leaders. These are some of the fundamentals of coaching football. But what are the fundamentals of your business?

- What behaviors are you trying to instill in your employees every day?
- How are you intentionally reinforcing those behaviors?
- How are you developing the core fundamentals of your organization?

TRUST

Like connection on the front end, trust holds up the entire framework. I challenge you to think not of trust simply, as in trusting others; instead, I empower you to focus on *earning* trust.

A great example of how I tried to earn trust as a coach comes from my early days as a coach. I remember I always preached accountability, but I didn't just talk about it—I lived it. One season, during an especially grueling stretch of practices, I made a promise to my group of guys. If they gave 100 percent effort every single day, I would be right there with them, pushing just as hard. At first, I didn't think much of it—coaches always say things like that. But then I noticed something: they were watching to see if I lived up to what I said. So I ran with them. I did the extra conditioning drills. If they were out in the freezing cold, so was I. If they stayed late watching film, I was in the room with them. I never asked them to do something I wasn't willing to do myself.

That's when trust was built—not through words, but through actions. I showed up for them, and in return, they showed up for me. As a coach, earning trust isn't about demanding respect or setting rigid rules. It's about consistency, accountability, and proving that you'll stand beside your team when it matters most. Trust isn't given; it's earned, little by little.

This concept of earning trust was formed early in my life, and I learned that to do so, my actions had to generate and reflect intentionality. As a leader, the flip side of this is just as powerful. You must learn to trust your people. Nothing moves us more than when people believe in us, and we feel valued and heard. Although, as leaders, we try to earn trust, the best leaders empower their team by trusting them. The same principle of gaining trust can apply to your troops.

I am talking about how your team perceives that you trust them. Do you micromanage them? Do you look over their shoulder? Or do you give them the freedom and autonomy to create what they need to make? Do you give them the flexibility to complete the job as they see fit, even though it may not be how you would do it? Do you trust and convey the trust that they will figure things out just as you have?

Somewhere along the way, somebody gave you the freedom or the flexibility to figure it out. I am not saying you can do this with every single employee, but to be the most effective leader, you better do it with a large percentage of them. Trust is empowering. It builds character and creates motivation. If I walk into a workplace, I can tell within three minutes of talking to an employee whether or not it's an environment built on trust.

The last lens I want you to look through in this area is how to handle the employees when you do not feel like you can trust them. There will always be team members who don't yet have your best interests at heart, and you must handle them accordingly. Lack of trust can erode and force you to make changes you may not want to make. If you are unwilling to deal with challenging scenarios where a change needs to be made, you will erode trust with all the people with which you worked so hard to build.

When you go through your checklist and ask yourself if you trust someone, I challenge you to first ask yourself if you've earned that person's trust. Those two questions must be answered hand in hand.

A FINAL NOTE ON LEADERSHIP

Leadership isn't just about decisions and expectations—it's about connection, trust, and intentionality. The CRUSH-IT framework helps leaders create cultures that inspire, unify, and elevate those around them. True leadership starts with deep, meaningful connection, requiring vulnerability, authenticity, and a genuine interest in people. The best leaders don't just manage; they unify, fostering a "we over me" mentality that separates great teams from average ones. Without connection, trust cannot exist, and without trust, leadership falls apart.

Trust isn't demanded—it's earned through consistent action, accountability, and empowerment. Great leaders extend trust, fostering autonomy and ownership while maintaining a clear plan for connection, culture, and growth. Without intentionality, teams rely on performance metrics instead of meaningful relationships. Those who truly crush it don't just set the standard—they live it daily, leading with integrity, empowering their teams, and building success on trust, respect, and a shared mission.

So, I'll leave you with this challenge: What is your plan for connection? What is your process for trust? How will you show up—not just in words, but in actions? Because leadership isn't about the moments when things are easy—it's about what you do when it's hard, when it's uncertain, and when it matters most.

CONCLUSION

Now that you have a framework for what crushing it looks like, the real challenge begins. The goal is for you to take *The CRUSH-IT Formula* and apply it to an area of your life where you need it most. What I love about this concept is that, as we define what crushing it looks like, we create a powerful tool to push ourselves forward. So, what does crushing it mean for you as a parent, an athlete, or an employee? What does it mean for your children, your teammates, or your colleagues?

The power lies in your ability to define the principles that matter most to you. And while the challenge is fitting those values into *The CRUSH-IT Formula*, I have faith that you're creative enough to do it.

MEASURING SUCCESS WITH INTENTIONALITY

When we started this journey, we talked about how people often use the wrong measuring tools. True change requires consistency. Long-term success isn't about quick wins but about sustained effort and intentional daily habits. But how do you know if you're truly showing up as your best self? Often, we feel it in our gut, but feeling isn't enough. You need a way to measure progress, track growth, and hold yourself accountable.

Whether you use *The CRUSH-IT Formula* or create your own acronym, this tool helps you apply intentionality in key areas of your life. For example, if I'm crushing it as a dad, my acronym might be Care, Responsibility, Unselfishness, Support, and Happiness. If I'm crushing it in my workouts, my acronym might be Consistency, Reliability, Unwavering Discipline, Strength, and Healthy Habits. Your acronym becomes a measuring stick for success.

NOW IT'S YOUR TURN

I challenge you to email me and share your CRUSH-IT model. Does it focus on supporting others? Is it about seeking coaching and developing high-performance habits? What do you need to do to elevate your game?

Imagine yourself like the little girl in that picture, reaching up to the sky, declaring, "I'm going to crush it today!" This isn't just a framework—it's your starting point, and now, it's time to put it into action. Define your highest self. Step up. Show up. Impact the world. Leave your mark. Unleash that unstoppable identity inside you. Develop the resilience you need to chase your biggest dreams. Have the courage to declare who you are and what you're about to achieve. Show up daily with discipline, tenacity, and a mindset that overcomes every challenge.

We all have incredible potential, but potential alone isn't enough. It's about performance. It's about daily action. It's about giving yourself permission to fulfill your greatest destiny. And most importantly, it's about having the right tools to track, measure, and refine your performance. Now that you have them, I'm with you every step of the way. Join our community, and now, go attack.

Go CRUSH-IT!

THANK YOU FOR READING MY BOOK!

Just to say thanks for buying and reading my book, I would like to give you a free introduction call, no strings attached!

Scan the QR Code:

I appreciate your interest in my book and value your feedback as it helps me improve future versions of this book. I would appreciate it if you could leave your invaluable review on Amazon.com with your feedback. Thank you!

www.ingramcontent.com/pod-product-compliance
Lightning Source LLC
Chambersburg PA
CBHW032041090426

42744CB00004B/87